CW01558854

SO IT'S TOUGH
OUT THERE, IS IT?

A parable for people in business

Barry Durdant-Hollamby

THE ART
of
CHANGE

Content copyright © Barry Durdant-Hollamby 2006

First Published in the United Kingdom by
The Art of Change
PO Box 441
East Grinstead
West Sussex RH18 5DH
www.artofchange.co.uk
email: welcome@artofchange.co.uk

ISBN 09530063-3-6
978 0 953 0063 3 5

A Cataloguing-in-Publication record for this book
is available from the British Library

All rights reserved. The contents of this book may not be reproduced
or transmitted in any form or by any means without written
permission of the publisher.

All characters in this publication are fictitious and any resemblance to
real persons, living or dead, is purely coincidental.

Cover artwork:
Ian Sishton and David Brown

Cover photograph:
Christine Balderas

Typesetting:
David Brown, Maynards Green, Heathfield, Sussex TN21 0DG.

Printing and binding:
Lightning Source Uk Ltd.
www.lightningsource.com

"Success in any endeavor depends on the depths to which it is an expression of your true self."

(unknown)

1

"Crap!"

Brenda was having another difficult morning. The Phillips' deal had only just been closed and already there were problems and hey, guess what, the problems were all about a failure on the tech side again.

Brenda was in her late twenties, a strong girl with what many people from a certain generation would describe as a good backbone. She was the first voice you heard at Straight-Talking Finance Ltd and the first face you saw. She had honed her greeting skills to such an extent that, up until recently, she had generally managed to calm down the most irate of clients within a few sentences.

But over the last few months she had found her abilities had waned a little as her patience had worn thin. It seemed like the same issues were coming up time and time again. The personnel might have changed a bit in that time, but the problems seemed to remain the same. And Terry, who she had once

1

thought of as being the most responsible member of Sales, seemed to have become as thoughtless and brash as everyone else.

He wasn't even in yet. It was his bloody champion on the phone having a shout and Terry wasn't even in yet. She couldn't exactly blame him, after all he was kept at work until 8.30 last night because the Americans wanted to instil a bit of the old 'this is how late we work in America' ethos into the UK work-force. Of course, no-one bought it, but everyone made the right noises.

So, there she was, having to palm off/sweet-talk/lie to yet another disgruntled client when a man walked in who was about to change her life. In fact not only her life but also the lives of everyone in the UK office. And the European offices. And ultimately even the Americans.

Of course Brenda wouldn't realise that until quite a while after this man had long disappeared from her orbit.

2

Brenda finished her sweet-talking act on the phone just as a man wearing an open shirt, jacket and chinos entered the reception area of Straight-Talking Finance Ltd. He walked up to the reception desk and reached out his hand in a greeting, a gesture Brenda found a little disconcerting. She hadn't touched anyone in the office since last year's Christmas party.

"Hello. You must be Brenda." He was quietly spoken and there was something peaceful in his manner.

Brenda looked quickly at the appointments diary. Nothing. No outside visitors expected for another hour. She hated not being in control of things and immediately assumed one of the boys must have forgotten to enter this one in. Left out of the loop again, nothing new there then.

Brenda's world-famous smile accompanied her reply.

"Good Morning Mr..." she left a gap which most visitors would have filled straightaway. But not this one. He let her words hover in the ether. Before he said anything Brenda continued.

"I don't appear to have your name here in the diary. Who are you here to see Mr...?"

He spoke with a certainty that only the very successful ever seem to possess. "Most people just call me Coach. And don't worry Brenda, I'm not in your diary. But I should be, because I'm here to talk to you first."

Brenda was thrown completely off her guard. The only people who ever came to see her were the office supplies deliverers and the caterers. Not that she couldn't have dealt with half the visitors that the business attracted; she did after all have a degree in business studies. Anyway the opportunity had never arisen.

"Me? What does a coach want to talk to me about?" She could feel her stomach turning over and her lips and mouth drying up instantly as she tried to work out why a business coach would be interested

4

in her. Had the company had a complaint about her efficiency? Had the Americans disliked her style during their visit?

"Brenda, let me ask you a question. What would be the best thing that could happen to you at work this week?"

3

"The Americans sent you over didn't they?"

The Coach didn't say a word. He remained smiling and peaceful. Brenda knew straightaway that the Americans had instigated this and she also knew that if her CEO James Duncan wasn't in on it—which at that time she couldn't believe he was— James would hit the roof. He hated it when the Americans presumed to know how best to run a European business. Goddamit during their recent visit the COO had even confessed not to know whether Scotland had a different currency from England. Having been born just outside Dundee,

Duncan had been less than pleased.

Well, nothing Brenda could do right now other than to answer the question. James was away until mid-afternoon and the Americans wouldn't be in their Seattle office for another few hours yet. And besides which, she found that there was something quite compelling and appealing about the presence of the Coach. He just seemed like a nice bloke, so why shouldn't she answer.

"Okay. So your question was what would be the best thing that could happen to me this week at work—right?" The Coach nodded. Brenda stayed silent this time and reflected for a minute.

"Well it would be very nice if I didn't get hassled by one client this week." She paused for another moment and allowed herself to feel what that would be like. "Oh yeah, now that would be great."

The Coach smiled. "Okay Brenda, that's a good start. Now think a bit further. Is there anything you can do to give this the best chance of happening?"

"Yep, I could refuse to answer the phone."

Brenda and the Coach allowed themselves a laugh; she was lightening up by the minute and beginning to enjoy the feeling of dealing with no distressed clients. It had been a long time since she could remember as much as 48 hours going by in the office without a major complaint and the usual fire-fighting that would follow it.

"Well since I apparently don't know enough to deal with the clients on anything other than a super-ficial level, I suppose I'm powerless to stop them ringing so there's no point in going down that route."

The Coach nodded in agreement.

"So if there is anything else I can do I'm damned if I know what it is."

The Coach prompted her. "Well let's see now. Does anyone here know how you feel about having to deal with all this shit?"

Brenda felt surprised for some reason at his use of this profanity. And yet somehow the word sounded different when it came out of his mouth. It took on a quality of meaning that made her squirm a bit at the realisation that this was precisely what she

7

was doing on a daily basis; dealing with other people's shit. All of a sudden she felt more like a bog-cleaner than an office administrator.

She felt relieved when the switchboard went and she had to answer a call which she put straight through to 'Jovial Julian' in Accounts. She had her own private nicknames for everyone; it helped her to stay sane.

The Coach repeated his question, a little more subtly this time. "Brenda, does anyone here know how you feel about having to deal with disgruntled clients so often?"

"Well, yes and no. I mean sometimes I let off steam when a client is really being a pain and then I guess everyone hears me. But generally I just take it out on the computer keyboard or coffee machine."

The Coach was in sight of his first goal. "Brenda, how would you feel if you had just told everyone here that you're really pissed off at having to spend so much time apologising for their mistakes and pretending they aren't available to talk when they're no more than 20 yards away from you?"

Brenda's pupils nearly doubled in size. "If I could say that I'd feel absolutely fantastic." She paused for a moment and her eyes returned to normal. "And absolutely terrified."

The Coach looked kindly at her from the other side of the reception desk. "Brenda, welcome to the art of change."

4

Terry Johnson was woken up by the phone ringing in his ear. He reached out with his left hand and swept it off the coffee table beside him.

"Terry, it's Mick. You found the phone then. Sorry mate but you looked out of it when I left the flat this morning so I thought I'd give you an alarm call once I'd got into work."

Terry's mouth felt dry and stuck together. "Shit. What time is it Mick?...Bollocks. Thanks mate—appreciate it—again."

Terry dropped the phone onto the floor and slid

off the couch where he had slept. What was this now, the third week? The fourth week? He had to get something sorted soon, sleeping like this wasn't doing him any bloody good at all.

So, late for work again. Very, very late. Still the Americans had gone and there would only be the accounting, media and tech teams in this morning since the rest of the sales team were out at various appointments. And, thank God, Duncan wasn't due in until much later.

"Going to have to tell someone sometime" he reasoned to himself. Things had been going pear-shaped with Tara for months, but it had finally blown up a few weeks back when she'd thrown him out for failing to remember Joel's fourth birthday party. No-one at work knew yet—well you don't take your stuff to work do you—but he knew that he couldn't carry it on for much longer.

What killed him about it was the boys. Two under 5, Joel and Brett. Now he was reduced to weekend visits whilst Tara was 'getting her head together'. Not that he'd had much time for them during the week when he was living at home, but at least he felt he could see them if he wanted to. Now he was a time-tabled parent and he didn't like it. Terry had been totally unprepared for how much he'd miss his sons.

He hated it when his morning started like this. Late for work and hacked off about the split. He quickly got washed and dressed and pulled the door of the one-bed flat shut behind him.

He pulled out his mobile and switched it on. Once it had fired up he ran through the messages and texts, nearly walking straight into a pushchair which was being carefully guided along the middle of the pavement by a very serious looking young woman.

The woman shouted after him: "Mind out for God's sake." But Terry was already out of earshot, or at least he pretended to be.

He checked through the texts. More trouble. Amongst the crap from Tara about solicitors there were numerous panic texts from Brenda and François, head of the tech team, about the problems with the Phillips' solution that they had cobbled together to win the deal.

Well all that was for someone else to worry about, Terry reasoned to himself; his remit was to get business, not think about whether his company could then deliver. Those tech boys, they all worry too much. And Brenda? Well, she used to be okay when everything was going well but since the pressure had increased it was becoming clearer to Terry that she just didn't understand how business really worked.

Half-running half-walking he carried on his way but he couldn't escape that slightly unsettled feeling he had in his stomach every time he thought about the Phillips' deal.

He made his way quickly to work—thank God for Mick's place. Just before he got out of the lift he checked his hair and face in the mirror, adjusted his tie and with his usual swagger entered the office.

He breezed past Brenda and barely noticed the stranger standing beside her as he went straight to his desk, put down his brief-case and went into the kitchen to get himself a coffee and a bowl of cereal.

The Coach spoke to Brenda quietly and calmly.

"Brenda this might be a good time to start practising telling people what you feel about fending off angry clients all the time. Always start with small steps and use this opportunity to let one person know about a situation you're not happy with in the present moment. It's your truth—come from your truth and you'll only ever get back even more good stuff. Try it. Trust me."

Brenda shuffled hesitantly on her chair. The phone went again. It was Terry's champion at Phillips screaming blue murder. She put him on hold.

"Terry." No answer. "TERRY." This time Terry came out of the kitchen, bowl of cereal in one hand and a large mug of black coffee in the other.

"It's John again at Phillips. There's a problem with the software and he wants to talk to you right now. He's been phoning since 8.30am."

Terry took a sharp intake of breath. He looked like a schoolboy that had just been found out at school for doing something wrong.

"Stall him. Tell him I'm in a meeting. I'll get back to him as soon as I've spoken to François.

Please?" Terry tilted his head to one side and gave Brenda a softening smile.

Brenda grimaced. She didn't look up at the Coach once during this exchange, the real world of business snapping her out of her thoughts of truth and honesty sharing. She put the call live again.

"Hello, yes Mr Alexander, I'm afraid Terry is in a meeting and can't be interrupted right now. He does know about the situation and is waiting for the technical team to respond. He says he'll call you no later than lunch-time today." Brenda listened while the voice at the other end of the phone expressed doubt and frustration. "Oh yes, I promise Mr Alexander. He'll call you by 12.30pm. Yes you can quote me on that. Me? Yes that's right I'm Brenda. Bye now, have a good day."

Brenda put the receiver down. She was anxious and angry. She suddenly remembered the Coach. She looked up expecting to see a disapproving look from him for failing to speak her truth.

But he was gone.

5

Julian Miller had just put down the phone when he looked up to see a stranger hovering around his territory. His two assistants hadn't noticed him which was weird since they were closer to him than Julian.

"Can I help you?" Julian asked in his usual inquisitive way.

"Good morning Julian." The Coach held out his hand—"and thank you, yes you can help. I'm here to see you."

Julian shook hands and looked down at his desk. "Er, right. Let me see. No, I've nothing down in my diary. May I ask your name?"

"Oh you can just call me Coach. Brenda knows all about me. I'm here to help you Julian."

"Help me with what exactly?" Julian replied defensively. He didn't like being told that he needed help, he prided himself on being able to run an accounts team which was hyper-efficient. He'd been with the company since it had started in the UK in '94

15

and knew everything that anyone could know about its UK finances.

The Coach looked at him knowingly. "Julian, if there was one problem in life right now that you could fix, what would it be?"

Julian became even more defensive. "What sort of a bloody question is that?" is what he wanted to say. But he didn't. He was suddenly thinking about why was this man here and why was he asking a question like this. Had the Americans sent him under-cover to discover the weak links in the UK business? He did after all know his name.

Julian remembered something that Sven, the European CEO had said to him during their last conference call. Something about "you never know what's going to happen next in business so stay sharp." Was this that "next" thing?

He decided to engage with the stranger.

"This problem you're talking about fixing, you're talking about business right?"

The Coach looked at Julian and smiled. "I could be Julian. And on the other hand I might not be."

16

"Well, you're being paid by the company. We're here on company time and I'm sitting in the company's office on a company chair. So I'm going to assume this has to relate to company stuff. Right?"

"Totally logical Julian. And that's why you're head of accounts. But wrong." The Coach picked up a piece of blank paper and a pencil and drew a cube on it.

"See this Julian? What does it look like to you?"

Julian hesitated before answering, not wanting to give the wrong reply.

"A box?" he offered hopefully.

The Coach smiled "That's right Julian, a box. And that's just what we've got to get you thinking outside of right now."

The Coach paused whilst Julian shuffled uncomfortably in his seat. The Coach continued.

"So think about it Julian. If there was one problem—ANY PROBLEM—that you could fix in life right now what would it be?"

"And it doesn't have to do with accounts, my assistants, my CEO, software solutions…?"

The Coach answered calmly. "Only if one of those represents the biggest problem in life right now Julian."

Julian leant a little further over his desk. The Coach could see his eyes welling up a little. Julian took the pencil and on the outside of the box that the Coach had drawn he wrote 'my kid?'

The Coach looked at him and nodded his head. He spoke very quietly. "What is it about your child that's a problem Julian?"

Julian again took the pencil and wrote on the paper the word 'drugs'. He was a very private man and did not want anyone else in the office knowing that his only child had a drugs problem that was beginning to run away with his life. The boy had recently been given a final warning by his school. One more slip and that would be expulsion.

"What time are you giving this problem at the moment Julian?" The Coach's question was simple and direct.

For all Julian's British reserve he jumped upon this opportunity to talk about the issue that had been tearing him apart. He'd been desperate to talk to someone about it yet somehow could never quite do it. Certainly no-one at work would be interested and anyway what would they think? And he hated the idea of going to see a therapist. He'd seen one once about 15 years ago when he was panicking about being a father. All the bloke did was listen. Julian wanted solutions.

He stood up and motioned to the Coach to follow him. They went into the White Room and the Coach shut the door. Julian sat down at the small shiny table, put his face in his hands and took a deep breath.

6

"You do solutions right? Because I'm not really interested in just gabbing away for an hour and then coming away with no clues as to what to do." Julian got the words out quickly and nervously.

"Well, I don't exactly have your answers Julian,

19

no." The Coach left a pause for these words to filter through before continuing. "But experience tells me that you do have all the answers you'll ever need. All I have to do is get you asking the right questions. I can't ask you to believe that yet, but I would ask you to be open to the possibility."

Julian was quiet. The Coach repeated his initial question. "So tell me, what time are you giving this problem at the moment Julian?"

Julian had already been considering his answer. "I haven't really been giving it—him—time. I've been letting my wife get on with it but she hasn't got a clue what to do any more. I've been burying myself in work, hoping it will go away but it seems to be getting worse." His eyes were watering quite clearly by now. The Coach handed him a paper tissue.

The Coach remained quiet. Julian continued. "I feel such a—such a bloody failure. I've worked my arse off in this place to provide everything he could ever want and look what I have to show for it. A son that's getting hooked on drugs and who hates my guts."

"Does he?" The Coach asked with genuine interest. "Does he really hate your guts. How do you know that? I mean for sure? Can you be 100% certain that there isn't something else going on here?"

Julian looked up from his hands. "What sort of thing do you mean?"

"Julian how well do you know him? I mean really know him? How old is he, 15–16?" Julian nodded his head. "When was the last time the two of you did anything together? You know, just for fun? When was the last time you shared with him how it feels to work so hard for your family only to have your family reject you? How much does he know about what you want from your life? And how much do you really know about what inspires him and who he really wants to be?"

Julian looked at the Coach as if he was speaking a different language. He'd never once thought about sharing his feelings and problems with his kid. Apart from anything else his son never showed any interest in his work, so why should he tell him? What would be the point?

The Coach second-guessed him. "You might be surprised at the reaction you'd get if you just let him into your life a little bit. Could it be possible that you know virtually nothing about him because you've told him virtually nothing about yourself? Could it be that he is just mirroring your own behaviour?"

"But he hates everything to do with accountancy and maths. He's very bright at it but he detests it. Only the other day he said that the worst thing that could happen in life is if he ended up being like me. That hurts you know." Julian took off his glasses with his left hand and with his right hand he rubbed his face.

"But Julian are you really just an accountant and a mathematician? Don't you have other passions and desires?" The Coach let Julian think about this before carrying on.

"Julian I want to ask you another question. I've got a magic wand here." Julian looked at him somewhat quizzically as the Coach waved his empty right hand in the air.

"This magic wand makes anything possible—

even things that right now seem totally unlikely. I want you to imagine that we've just jumped forwards three months. It's October 1st and you have just spent the most incredible three months of your parenting life where you have established an amazing relationship with your son and where you have been totally there to share parenting responsibilities with your wife.

"You've opened up to your son the struggles you face as a man and a father and you've told him what you dream about happening in the future. You've told him about some of the things that you'd love to do if only you had the time to do them, and about some of the things you wish you'd never done.

"You've been able to ask him about his drugs and he's been able to confide in you why he feels the need to use them. You've been able to accept that he's got different interests and you've also found that there are some things you enjoy sharing together. And your wife has, for the first time maybe in years, felt like she was really sharing the most important of all jobs. That of being a parent.

"If this was all able to happen how do you think you would be feeling come October 1st, Julian?"

Julian had listened attentively throughout the Coach's monologue. He put his hands together and reeled off a list of adjectives.

"Inspired, light, relieved, amazed, excited…"

The Coach smiled. Julian cried. The Coach continued: "Julian this is your truth. It's a word which most people don't understand. In fact quite a few people find it extremely threatening. And yet the embracing of it enables each one of us to function at much closer to our highest potential. So here's another question for you Julian. What stops you from embracing this truth?"

Julian wiped his eyes and gathered his thoughts together before answering. "Well, where would I start? And isn't it too late, I mean he's nearly 16?"

The Coach answered clearly and firmly: "It's never too late to start being who you really are. In fact the only time to start is right now. Now is the place where the miracles happen Julian. As for how you could start? Well here's another radical concept for you. Whatever you want more of in life, start giving it first. You want better communication with your son, start communicating better with him. You want better, happier family time start aiming to create more and happier family moments. This ain't rocket-science Julian, it's logic. You're a logical man—you should be good at this."

Julian looked up at the Coach and asked a question that he thought might catch out this stranger who, in the space of just a few moments, had shaken his world to its very roots. "But how, pray tell me, is all this going to help me to improve my performance at work? I mean, excuse me if I'm wrong, but going back to business for a moment we're here on company time in a company room—how is what you're suggesting going to help the company? What you're suggesting will mean me working a more normal day and therefore spending less time at work. They'll be getting less of me. And then I'll be put under more pressure to make up the time I've lost."

The Coach nodded his head. "Yep, you've got a point there Julian."

"Hah" said Julian triumphantly. There was a pause in which he felt a certain smugness at his managing to stem the flow of the Coach's confidence.

The Coach put his hands together almost as if he were praying. "Let's see if we can make some sense of all this. Answer me a couple more questions Julian first if you would. How would you judge your performance has been over the last say 18 months in comparison to your previous 5 years?"

Julian shifted uncomfortably. He hesitated before answering. "Well, it hasn't been totally brilliant—but there are reasons—and I'm getting back on track now." Suddenly Julian was scratching around in the truth of his present situation and trying to pluck some positives.

"It's okay Julian, you don't have anything to prove to me. Now answer me this: how do you think your performance would be affected if your home situation was balanced and calm—maybe even, dare

I say it, fun and exciting?"

"Well, I guess, I guess it would be better."

The Coach was in his element. "You guess it would be better? Or you know it would be better?"

Julian looked away for a second; somehow the Coach's piercing stare was too much for him. "Okay. Christ I know it would be better. Tons better. I perform crap when things are screwed up at home. But I try not to. It just, it just happens."

"Of course it does Julian. It happens to everyone, you are not alone. How often have you heard the expression 'leave your domestic problems at home where they belong, don't bring them to work'. Well I'd love to meet the man who invented the tool that meant you could put things out of your mind, he must be very rich by now. If he exists. What do you think Julian? Do you think he exists?"

Julian shook his head.

"Of course he doesn't exist. You can't put things out of your mind. You will bring your domestic problems to work. You can't excise them from your mind. Worries will continue to bother you regardless of your geographical situation. What we have to do is help to solve the problems. You see Julian, come into work on a Monday morning feeling great about who you've been as a dad, lover, partner over the weekend and the likelihood is you will perform great. Come into work feeling crap about who you've been at the weekend and you will perform crap. It ain't rocket-science. And it does work."

Julian had another question: "And working shorter hours?"

"Julian, you need to work smarter not longer. Do the hours that are expected of you. Most people, if they are functioning clearly and able to concentrate purely on the job in hand, could get an average 10 hours work done in 5 hours. A massive amount of time is wasted through tiredness and stress. Poor decision-making and error-ridden reports are just two common results of people who work too hard. You don't get thanked for working longer hours— you get thanked for producing the right results. Focus on removing the stress in your life, wherever it's coming from, and you will start working far

28

smarter."

Julian weighed up what the Coach had said. He replied thoughtfully and clearly. "Okay Coach, I get it. I'm willing to hear more. Where do we start?" Julian's voice was sounding lighter. His body language had changed from the closed almost squirming state at the beginning of the meeting to a more open and welcoming position.

The Coach laughed. "Ah yes, the logical mind at work. Once you start to get results with this you will fly Julian because you'll put the equation together. You'll know that by changing this and adjusting that you produced such and such a result. Okay, well here's the good news. You haven't got to do anything big."

Julian let out another sigh of relief. The Coach continued.

"Look to take the smallest of small steps. Don't look to create massive change straight away, you won't sustain it. The first thing I think you need to do is to honour the idea that you want to change the way in which you relate to your family. This will help you to look for opportunities to bring this into reality. Don't try to do it all at once. Maybe start by sitting down with your wife tonight and sharing that you want to support her more and share the responsibility more equally. How would that feel Julian if you had just had a conversation with her along those lines?"

Julian smiled. "Fantastic."

"Well, there you go—that's guidance then isn't it? Maybe you could take another small step by leaving a little earlier tonight and getting home at a reasonable time to have supper with them both as well."

"Supper? Together? Wow—we haven't done that since Kieran's birthday in February. He'd think something was up."

"Well Julian, he'd be right. Something is up. And hopefully a lot more will be up after a couple of months of really honouring who you are."

Julian stood up in the sunlight that was now flooding the room and shook the Coach's hand. "Thank you. Thank you for reminding me who I am.

I appreciate that. Shall I send in someone else?"

"Well, you send in whoever you think would be the most appropriate Julian. And remember—the smallest of steps please. The mathematician inside you knows you can't just jump to the answer without going through the workings-out first. And you watch what happens over the next few weeks and months."

Julian felt several stone lighter as he left the White Room that morning. He headed straight for his desk where he called his wife to tell her she could expect him home in time for supper tonight.

He then went over to the tech team and told Matt Jenkins that the Coach was waiting to see him in the White Room. Matt looked up rather blankly at Julian but took the offer of relief from staring at his screen of numbers. He grabbed his Coke and wandered aimlessly over to the White Room. The Coach looked out of the window up at the sky and felt energised as the sun's rays lit up the room.

7

Matt walked in and muttered a barely discernable "hello" to the Coach. The Coach motioned to him to sit down.

"Hi Matt. How's it going?" Matt didn't think for a minute that it was odd that the Coach knew exactly who he was. Once you're employed *they* all know everything about you.

"Alright". Matt never used more words than he had to. He wasn't big on talking and never had been. "So what's all this about then?" Matt looked across at the Coach and for a moment made eye-contact before quickly looking away again. In that second the Coach understood that Matt was in some sort of emotional pain.

"Matt, I've got a question for you. If there was one quality you could develop that would help you to achieve what you really want to achieve—what would it be?"

Matt looked down at the floor. "Dunno" he

muttered under his breath.

"Matt, think about it. There's stuff going on in your life right now that is bugging the hell out of you. You need to develop new qualities to be able to change these things. What quality would you choose to help you to transform your present circumstances?"

Matt contemplated the question. He was a bright young man, quick thinking but incredibly shy. The Coach knew that if he could get Matt to trust him just a bit he could open up big-time.

"Is this being recorded or anything?"

The Coach shook his head. "God no, they couldn't afford my recording fees Matt." The two men laughed.

Matt started picking a nail on his hand. The Coach sensed that Matt was struggling with the idea of unburdening something big to someone he barely knew. He waited. Matt put his hand up to his mouth and started chewing the same nail.

"Well, the thing is—now this is nothing to do with work mind you—I'm getting married next month."

The Coach smiled. "Congratulations Matt. That's great."

Matt replied quickly. "That's the problem. It's not great. Now that the wedding is getting closer, I'm not sure I want to get married at all." Matt breathed out a huge sigh. He rubbed his finger where he had been biting it. The Coach remained silent.

"My fiancée has been going on and on about getting married for ages and I didn't want to let her down, we got drunk one night and I proposed. But I really, truly don't think I can marry her. And I also haven't been able to tell her because she's going to be totally gutted. And then there's her family, my family, our friends…" Matt looked up at the Coach. "You see, I told you this had nothing to do with work."

The Coach now understood the pain that he had seen in Matt's eyes earlier. He also understood why Matt was having a problem looking anyone in the eye—he didn't want to look life right in the eye at the moment that was for sure.

"Okay Matt, good one. Nothing minor then?" Matt laughed again, this time almost despairingly.

34

The Coach continued. "Thanks for sharing this. And yes, it relates entirely to work. People round here are going to start figuring out pretty soon that if your life outside of work is in a state of anxiety and confusion, your life at work will mirror this. Tell me, how would you say your performance at work has been in the last couple of months?"

Matt felt uncomfortable at this question. He wanted to say how difficult he had been finding it to concentrate, how nothing seemed particularly inspiring at the moment, how fed up he was getting with not being listened to by the head of the tech team and how pissed off he was getting with being blamed for anything related to the company's technical solutions going wrong. But he was afraid of sharing information which might be used against him by the company.

He made eye contact with the Coach again. Something made him want to trust him.

"Okay. The truth is my performance hasn't been good. In fact, I'd say I've been keeping my head down hoping that no-one would notice. But I guess I can't get away with that can I? Someone has noticed haven't they?"

The Coach said nothing. Matt continued.

"There's a load of reasons why and they're not all to do with the fact that I'm not ready to get married. I'm fed up because whenever something goes wrong with the tech solutions, François ends up having a go at me in front of everyone else, even though most of the time it's not been my fault." Matt took a deep breath before continuing. He'd never spoken so openly about work before. He'd never realised he felt so strongly about it.

"I'm also demotivated because François never listens to any of my ideas for developing a new database and customer log which I know would take a load of the heartache out of the present communications. In fact, I reckon it would make the company function loads more efficiently and gain us new clients."

The Coach noticed how Matt's body language was changing as he spoke. He was becoming more animated, more alive, as he spoke about the things that he'd like to see change.

"Matt, the question I asked you was what quality you'd like to develop more of in yourself to help you achieve your goals. Quite often people don't know what their goals are, but you seem to have some pretty clear targets already. Let's just make sure you're totally clear on these first.

"I want you to imagine that you have just sat down with your girlfriend and told her that you are not ready to make such a big commitment yet in life. How do you feel?"

Matt breathed out and smiled. "Relief." He paused. "Huge relief."

The Coach continued. "Matt when an answer comes back that quickly I would suggest that it's worth paying attention to. I'd call this your inner guidance or your intuition. It tends to come through before the intellect—your brain—has had a chance to edit the answer and bring in all the 'buts'. I've learnt to trust this guidance implicitly. And I reckon you could do a lot worse than do the same. At the very least you need to give yourself permission to consider having that conversation."

Matt was thoughtful, running over the implications of this new possibility in his mind. He'd never even thought of pulling out of the wedding. His mind became alive with the implications, both positive and negative.

The Coach continued. "Okay Matt, rest with that one for a bit. Let's move on to what's happening in your business life. You're learning skills now that could help you to become very successful in the future. One of those skills you need to learn is how to manage people.

"For whatever reason Matt, you and François have a problem with each other. In my book that potentially makes him a great teacher for you. He's bringing up your stuff—there's gold to gain from this. It sounds like François is showing you how not to manage people. For instance belittling colleagues in front of others is an absolute no-no. It's something that belongs in the pages of Tom Brown's Schooldays. You have heard of Tom Brown haven't you Matt?" The Coach suddenly realised Matt may never have come across the horrendous tale of life in a boys' boarding school.

"Vaguely. I think I remember seeing part of a TV series when I was a kid."

The Coach resumed his thread. "Great. Well, unbelievably there are still quite a few 'leaders' in business who use similar tactics to the teachers and prefects of Tom Brown's days. One of those tactics is public ridicule. The fact that it happens in plush offices and amongst people earning high salaries doesn't make it any less damaging or offensive. The best thing you can do is try to remove yourself from the situation.

"So the next time you become aware of François starting to have a go in public, ask him directly if you could discuss this one-to-one and in private. That may be his way of dealing with failure or mistakes, don't let it become your way. Go off to a quiet room, hear what he has to say, acknowledge his version of events and then, if necessary, state your own truth.

"If he refuses to discuss it in private then just let

him have his rant and tell him that when he's ready you'd be happy to discuss your version of events in private. Do not waver on this."

Matt had taken the pen out from behind his ear. "Can I just write this down Coach? I'm scared I might forget it." The Coach nodded his head and added "Don't worry Matt, you won't forget this stuff. But feel free to write what you want." Matt took a piece of paper from the computer printer beside the table and started writing. The Coach closed his eyes for a couple of minutes in quiet reflection.

When Matt had finished writing he looked up at the Coach who immediately opened his eyes again.

"Okay Matt, now about your thoughts for this business. I want you to imagine that you have laid out your ideas clearly for the database and client log and presented them to the CEO. How does that feel?"

Matt pondered this new question for a few moments. "Hmm, not sure on that one. Don't think I like the idea of going over François's head."

The Coach rephrased his question. "Okay

you've laid out your ideas in writing and presented them to François, how does that feel?"

Matt responded more quickly this time. "Yeah, that's better." Matt reflected for a moment. "But he won't go for it. I've mentioned them to him before and if it's not his idea he isn't interested. Or rather, if it's my idea he's not interested."

"That's fine Matt. Remember the question I started by asking you? What quality do you feel you most need to develop to achieve your goals? What quality do you think we are talking about here?"

Matt considered the question more carefully than ever. He thought about what had prevented him from sharing his true feelings with his girlfriend; he thought about what held him back from being clear with François when he knew his French IT head was wrong.

"Openness; courage; willingness to let people know what I think, rather than always being told what to do and what not to do by others." Matt's demeanour was changing with every word that he uttered.

"Matt you could sum them all up with one word. Truthfulness. I think it might be time to stop complying with everyone and everything, stop keeping your head down and start letting people know who Matt Jenkins really is. Don't you?

"You know, when you express a truth it's like sending out a boomerang into the universe. It tries to come back to you with a lot more of the same energy attached to it. When you come from your truth the same thing happens. A lot more of what you need to sustain that truth comes back to you.

"But remember one thing. Start by taking small steps first. With a big decision like the wedding give yourself at least 24 hours to consider what we've talked about before you do anything. Allow yourself to live with the idea for a bit first. Time is not an issue, it never is. But hurrying things often leads to greater problems. Let your truth grow."

Matt stood up in a mixed state of shock and euphoria. Twenty minutes ago he was getting married to a girl he didn't think he loved for reasons he couldn't quite fathom. Now he was giving himself permission to consider calling the whole thing off. His whole world felt transformed. This time it was Matt who reached out his hand to the Coach.

"Thanks man."

The Coach continued. "That's no problem Matt. Oh and when it comes to François, think about going round the desk and talking to him first to tell him you want to present the client log idea again. Don't be tempted to send an email, personal approaches work on an entirely different level from electronic communication. Hearts connect. It's much harder to ignore a personal approach."

"Whoa! Now that will be strange. Talking to him I mean. What the hell though. Nothing to lose really is there? Okay Coach, I'll give it a shot."

Matt looked directly at the Coach. He knew he had received in these few minutes some powerful information. Just how powerful, only time would tell. He got up to leave.

"Thanks again man, I, er, don't know what to say. I feel a bit weird."

The Coach beamed one of his biggest smiles.

"Thanks says it all Matt. Now go out there and have some fun. You do know life is meant to be fun don't you? Oh and pick someone else to come in will you?"

Matt walked out of the White Room, rushed straight into the washroom and let out a massive "Y-E-E-SSSSS" as he punched his fists into the air. He looked into the mirror and found himself making eye contact with himself. He liked the look of the man he saw staring back. He felt free. Life was never going to be the same again. That much he already knew.

8

"Wow. What's gotten into you?" asked Brenda as Matt came back into the office.

"Oh shit, did you hear that?" replied Matt, a grin stretching across his face. "I, er, just had some good news. Who should I send in to see him next Brenda?"

"Well he's seen me, Julian and you so far. What

44

about Shanti?"

Shanti was part of the PR and media team. Born in London to Indian parents, she was in her late twenties, as attractive as she was bright and was totally under-stretched by her current duties. Shanti could deconstruct a Thackeray novel, quote from Wordsworth, Shakespeare or Rowling and could even make the latest performance of a unit trust fund sound like the unveiling of the Oscars.

She had also been absent from work for a total of more than six months of her last year thanks to a series of colds, infections and fatigue type symptoms. Her CEO had stuck with her but even his patience was beginning to wear a little thin. And there would be only so much longer this could continue without people crying out that she was receiving 'favoured' treatment.

Matt—who had always been friendly with Shanti and felt some degree of empathy with her— went over to her desk and told her about the Coach in the White Room. She finished an email she was just writing and dutifully sent it. She then tidied up a pile of papers on her desk, reached for her bottle of spring water, picked up her pen and pad and walked into the White Room.

"You wanted to see me?" she asked as they shook hands.

"Yes, yes that would be good. Is now a good time?" asked the Coach.

"As good a time as any," replied Shanti as she sat down. "How can I help?"

"It's Shanti, isn't it? So who are you today Shanti?"

This question totally threw her. Not that the Coach meant to try to catch her out, it was just a line that he often used with people and he thought nothing of it these days.

"Who am I today? What an interesting question. Mr, er?"

"Coach. Just call me Coach. That will be fine"

"Okay well I suppose today I'm having a good morning. I didn't wake up feeling too tired and I've just finished the monthly newsletter and Russell isn't in this week so that helps me a little—he's head of media by the way did I tell you that, well you probably know anyway—and…"

Shanti went on without drawing breath. The Coach listened as attentively as he could, but it was just too much information. He held his hand up gently to bring Shanti's stream of consciousness to an end.

"That's great Shanti" he began, but Shanti interrupted at once. "Yes but what you don't know is that I'm also meeting today with Frenfall's PR team over lunch. We're going to look at the idea of putting together a bi-monthly publication for the whole IFA market."

"Okay Shanti, you've clearly got lots going on. You must have a lot of energy."

Shanti looked quizzically at the Coach. "I wish." For the first time she paused after her sentence.

"Have you not got a lot of energy Shanti? You don't seem to pause for breath, you're clearly creating new things all the time. You must have a lot of energy to be like you are, surely?"

47

Shanti reflected for a moment.

"Need a lot of energy, yes. Have a lot of energy—no. I've spent 6 months of the last year fretting in bed, sometimes unable to muster enough strength to get out of bed to make a cup of tea. I spent December in a wheelchair things were so bad. My parents were worried sick about me. I'm in a better cycle at the moment but I know it's just a cycle and at some point it will come to an end and I'll be laid up again."

Shanti was in full-flow again. "And next time I'm off, well I can't expect the company to put up with this forever. So in reference to your question, who I am today and most days is also someone who is terrified that they're permanently on the threshold of losing their job."

"And what would that mean to you Shanti? Losing your job I mean?"

"Failure. Loss of money and lifestyle and freedom. I get paid well here and the money gives me a certain amount of freedom to do what I want. Fear. How would I live? Would I be able to get another job as well paid as this? How much would my recent health track record count against me? What would people think of me?"

The Coach continued. "Okay, let's look at it from a different perspective. Tell me what it is about your job that inspires you?"

Shanti contemplated the Coach's latest question. "Well, when I joined, I thought I'd be doing a lot more travelling, writing up what our different overseas companies are up to. I'd also hoped to be doing a bit more TV and radio work than has transpired." Shanti paused for a minute.

"You know, thinking about it, I suppose I'm not feeling very inspired right now with it all. For one thing stress levels have increased over the last 18 months since the market has gone quiet. The CEO is always blaming someone for something. And me, well I'm just churning out much the same reports every month. I have no control over the eventual output anyway because Russell has the final say. I'm not getting any TV or radio work. I've put the bi-monthly publication idea together because I'm bored."

Shanti paused for a moment realising what she had just said. "I've never said that to anyone before. I'm really, really, bored. Is it alright to say this to you?"

"Of course Shanti, that is the whole point of this space. I want you to say what you are feeling, safe in the knowledge that nothing you want to remain confidential will be shared outside of here." His response reassured her and he asked Shanti another question.

"How long do you suppose you have been bored for Shanti?"

Shanti gave it some thought. "Well, I joined 18 months ago, I guess the first six months I was running on adrenalin just trying to find out what it was all about. I travelled round a bit more then as I had to meet up with the European branches to introduce myself. I guess the boredom set in about a year ago."

"So would you say the illness kicked in about the same time as the boredom?"

Shanti had never considered there was a link. Her face paled at the thought that flashed through her mind—that her physical condition could have had something to do with her mental state.

"The physical condition probably started within a month of my beginning to realise that I was not being stretched enough here, yes." She spoke more softly and slowly now.

The Coach was pleased to hear her becoming more reflective and speaking so honestly.

"According to my philosophy of life Shanti, it is entirely likely that your physical condition is mirroring your internal state. I'm not going to ask you to believe this but I would ask you to consider the possibility that stress of one kind or another is the source of all illness. You already know about the common stress caused by pressure of work, confrontational situations. For instance you've described having a boss who, when things aren't going perfectly, looks for someone to blame. Coming into an environment where that could happen to you at any time, where you could be on the receiving end

51

of his dissatisfaction, is immensely stressful. You can never quite relax. This type of management is meant to motivate, in fact it has the reverse effect. Ultimately it demotivates.

"But regular boredom and a lack of inspiring work on a daily basis is also stress. If you are feeling a lack of enthusiasm or inspiration for what you are doing every day, then it is entirely possible that your body will start to reflect that lack of enthusiasm for life. It is likely that *a daily struggle to get to work* is created by *a lack of desire for work*.

"The question we need to ask ourselves is this: Can you find inspiration in what you are doing?"

9

For once Shanti didn't have anything to say. She thought about the question the Coach had put forward. Inspiration? How could anyone find inspiration in trying to dress numbers up to look sexy? Because at the end of the day that's all she was doing.

Playing around every month with slightly different numbers and having to make them seem as fresh and interesting as possible.

"I'm not sure I like where this is taking me. I mean what you are saying to me basically is that my job is pointless. You are telling me that I should be able to find something inspiring about writing up finance. You try it. You try to be original month after month faced with some characterless figures and the same old conjectures. This business is not inspiring. It can't be. It is not in its nature"

Shanti was getting quite animated. She was angry. Angry with the Coach for pushing her out of her comfort zone and angry with herself for rising to the bait. The Coach looked on calmly.

"Shanti, I never said your job was pointless. Neither did I say that you 'should' be able to do anything. I simply asked if you could find inspiration within this job? That's quite different. You see, if we can help you to feel inspired, I've got a mad theory that your body will not feel it has to be dragged in to work everyday. If we can help you to feel inspired, I believe you will find your health problems could become a thing of the past. But all the time you feel bored, trapped and demotivated, your body will very likely continue to struggle as well."

Shanti looked straight into the Coach's eyes. "Are you telling me I may have to quit this job to regain my health?"

The Coach replied firmly. "I don't know. It's possible. Anything is possible. But it's also possible that we could help you to find inspiration right here, right now. It may seem unlikely at this moment, but sometimes just a change in perspective can bring about the most extraordinary results.

"It also helps if you can learn practical ways of dealing more effectively with stressful situations when they arise. A simple tool for instance such as taking a five minute time-out for some fresh air when you're feeling under pressure can work wonders for your clarity and strength."

Shanti's heart stopped pounding quite as fast as it had been. She began to feel a year's worth of discontentment being allowed to surface without, for once, demanding immediate solutions of herself. She'd known for ages that she couldn't go on like she was, but she couldn't think of any way of changing things without just walking out. And she didn't want to walk out yet. She liked the money, she liked some of the people, she liked the fact that this job would look great on her CV if she could hack it for a bit longer. And she valued the experience she had already gained in her time at STF Ltd.

She also liked the idea of gaining some practical ideas for improving her ability to deal with day-to-day pressures. "This sounds interesting Coach. Where do we begin?"

The Coach answered her confidently. "You've already begun Shanti. Just recognising where you are is a great start. In fact it's the only place to start. Okay, so you're in a job that isn't bringing you much joy and you've got a body that is continually letting you down. Is that a fair enough summing up of things right now?"

Shanti replied in the affirmative.

"Shanti, let's play a little game. Describe the

perfect working situation to me—your dream job."

Shanti was quick to reply. "Right, well, I'm getting paid a lot of money to write and to present TV shows." Shanti allowed herself a little laugh. The Coach smiled encouragingly.

"Anything else Shanti? What about the subject you're writing about or presenting? What about the people you're working with and the environment you're working in?"

"Right. Well I am using my writing and presentation skills to communicate information which is really useful to my audience. I am working in an environment which is uplifting and I am working with people who I respect and who respect me." She paused and reflected for a minute to contemplate this uplifting picture of life that she was painting.

"How am I doing?"

The Coach smiled again. "Well I'd say you're getting the hang of this. It sounds pretty good. Anything else?"

Shanti thought for a minute. "Well they are the most important things. At the risk of sounding like a beauty queen contestant I know I would like to be involved in a subject that could change the world. The environment or health for example. Something other than money anyway. Maybe something that could help people suffering back in India."

She looked the Coach directly in the eyes. "Money is such an unimportant issue in the great scheme of things."

"Is it?" asked the Coach perfectly seriously. "What makes you think money is so unimportant?"

"Well it is not like saving lives is it? Just people trying to make bigger profits, earn greater incomes, buy more expensive things. I should know, I'm one of them." Shanti's honesty sounded bitter in its tone.

"So is there no good side to money then Shanti?"

Shanti looked blank.

The Coach continued. "Shanti, it's possible that money is just another form of energy. Nothing more, nothing less. Money can be great, it can represent freedom, power and strength. It can of course also be misused—like anything can be—to control, hurt and weaken. It's all down to perspective. Choose to view money as the ultimate force of the devil and it will show its devil-like qualities. Choose to view it as a source of freedom and excitement and it will bring you that freedom and excitement."

The Coach was getting into his stride. "Now let's say that from what you've said so far you'd like to be doing a job that could make a difference in this world. Would that be right?"

Shanti nodded her head in agreement. The Coach continued: "Okay. Now I'm a great believer that we are in the perfect place at the perfect time. That we have the perfect tools around us now to start achieving what we are really here to do. Radical concept I know, but if you could just consider this as a possibility that'd be so good. Could you do that?"

"Well, I suppose I could consider it as a possibility. Although I find it hard to believe. I mean this place does not exactly seem perfect. If it was perfect, well we probably would not need someone like you coming in to sort our heads out would we?" Shanti just about managed a smile.

"Just so Shanti. But this is all down to perspective again. Right now there is nothing to stop you choosing to view everything that has happened in your life as being wrong. In the same way there is nothing to stop you from viewing everything as having happened just as it was meant to. It's down to the choice you make.

"You can choose to see life as being full of pain, illness, suffering etcetera etcetera or you can choose to view it as something that is full of challenges and opportunities. In the same way you can view working in money as being a worthless job compared to doing charity work or working as a nurse for instance; or you could view it as representing your greatest opportunity right now to do something good for the world."

"Okay Coach, now you are losing me. I see the point about how my attitude to my job is important, I understand what you say about the importance of feeling inspired. But how, oh how, can I possibly feel like I am making a difference in the world when I am working in the capitalist world of finance?" If Shanti had been a lawyer in court she would now have been resting her case. Here the Coach would surely be out of answers.

"It's a good question Shanti. A very good question. Let me ask you another one and see if we can turn this around. What group of individuals would most people say make the most important decisions in this world?"

Shanti didn't hesitate "Governments. Politicians."

"Yes, that's right. Governments. Organisations which are made up of politicians. Now how many politicians do you know who are on the breadline?"

"Well, none that I can name, not in this country anyway."

"And how do you think any of the leading political parties would fare if any of them showed themselves to be in financial dire straits?"

"Well voters probably would not trust them because they would think if they cannot keep their own business going how on earth could they keep the country's economy going."

"Exactly. So demonstrating wealth is also demonstrating power, efficiency and ability of some sort. So here's our first point. Having wealth can be useful in getting people to listen to you." Shanti scribbled down some notes on her paper.

The Coach carried on. "This one I hope helps you with any issue you might be having about what you earn. It could be that you'll get people to listen to you in the future partly because you come from a position of power.

"But let's go on to the more important point— the one about working in the world of finance and how that could relate to helping you achieve your vision of making a difference in the world." Shanti looked on, now intrigued with where the Coach could take this one.

"The world of finance contains some of the most important and influential decision-makers in the world. People who, right now, can really make a difference. For example, a decision to support a particular third world charity made by the annual charity steering group of a leading media or financial institution could change the course of thousands of lives. Not just tens or hundreds, but thousands, possibly even hundreds of thousands.

"You Shanti are working in this world. And you know how to communicate to these people. Not just to one or two of them in a meeting like we're having, but on the television or in a newspaper column where you could be reaching countless decision-makers.

"Where you are right now in your job is a place where miracles can happen. A place where, in the future, well who knows maybe you'll help to change the way that corporations use their profits, treat their staff and develop company strategy. Why? Because people listen to you. Your writing and presentation skills, when tied together with your desire to make a difference in the world, are unique. So here's the second point. You're in this financial world because this is the perfect place to begin making that difference."

Shanti was shuffling on her seat and writing away on her pad. Something the Coach was saying was stirring something inside her. She could feel excitement growing with every word and she could also sense the truth of what he was saying. She was in a powerful position. She was getting very well paid for her job. People did respect her.

She spoke, a little more slowly now than when she started the meeting. Now she was choosing her words more carefully. "So the more successful I become at what I am doing now, the greater my opportunity will be in the future to make a difference in the world?"

"Could be" replied the Coach. "But that doesn't mean that you don't just have to focus on becoming 'successful'. In fact, I'd replace the word 'successful' with the word happy. If you are happy with your work you'll be successful. The two are directly linked. Success is a much misunderstood term. For now all you need to know is that if you ain't happy at work, you sure as hell ain't successful at it."

Shanti took up the baton: "And being happy at work means feeling inspired by it; and the inspiration could be there every day by realising that where I am now is a stepping-stone towards achieving my goal which is to make a difference in the world."

Shanti was speeding up again, but this time with enthusiasm rather than nerves. She paused for a moment and then looked at the Coach as if something very major had just struck her.

"Oh My God. So I can go back to my desk and thank the financial reports and data sheets that I have because they are the very tools that are enabling me to live my dream."

"You've just made my third point for me" the Coach laughed.

Shanti sat back in her chair and contemplated the words that had just sprung unchecked from her mouth. There was no need to write this last point down, she had come up with it herself. She felt large weights lifting off her shoulders and from around her neck. She felt her head begin to clear and her breathing became more settled than she could remember it being in a long time. The Coach looked at her but she was busy staring wide-eyed out of the window. The penny had dropped. She would never be the same again.

10

As Shanti returned to her desk, in a daze as much as anything else, Brenda got up from her seat and entered the White Room.

"Can I get you a cup of tea, or a coffee or something?" The Coach was standing with his back to her looking up at the sky in between the high walls of the buildings opposite. He turned round, smiling:

"A glass of water would be great. Thanks Brenda. And when you come back you can tell me how it's going with that honesty."

Brenda went to get the glass of water. She felt pleased; she had wanted to go a bit deeper with this earlier conversation. Part of her was feeling guilty at not being able to be honest with Terry earlier and part of her was worried at him failing to get back in touch with the client and the client taking it out on her.

She decanted a large glass of cold water from the dispenser, asked Shanti to cover for her and walked back into the room where the Coach was now sitting down again. He thanked Brenda for the water and took a sip before addressing her.

"So, what did you find when you tried to share your truth earlier?" The Coach was direct and clear. Brenda felt somehow held and made safe by his confidence. This time she was much more able to be open.

"I just couldn't do it. I didn't want to upset Terry. He gave me that look of his and I just didn't want to land him in it." The Coach nodded his head, more in understanding with her than agreement.

"And what are the consequences of that action? How have you been feeling since?"

Brenda considered the question for a moment. "Well, I've been feeling a little anxious because I don't think Terry will do anything about this before lunch-time and when the client calls to find out what's happening, muggins here is going to be the one who answers the phone. And of course Terry will refuse to take the call. And I'm afraid that if the client gets angry with me I might say the wrong thing and I could end up blowing the whole account."

The Coach put his hand up gently to stop

Brenda's flow of worry.

"And what would have happened do you suppose if you had insisted that Terry take the phone call?"

"Well, Terry would have had to deal with it I suppose."

The Coach continued "And how would you be feeling now if Terry had had to deal with it?"

"Less anxious. Less angry and resentful towards Terry. Maybe a little sheepish that I had forced him to deal with it. But then I'd feel good as well because he has got to take responsibility for his clients. That's what he gets paid for after all. They're not my job."

Brenda was beginning to connect with a powerful feeling. For the first time this morning she could take a deep breath. She was imagining the thought of Terry taking responsibility for his clients and how much pressure that would take off her. She was soon imagining everyone taking responsibility for their clients and jobs. It was almost too peachy to contemplate.

"It's Terry's fault isn't it? I shouldn't be dealing with this at all, he should be." For a moment the Coach thought he saw a look of almost demonic power flash across Brenda's eyes.

"No Brenda it's not Terry's fault. And there are no 'shoulds' or 'should nots' either. This is not about blame or who did what wrong. And it's not about people doing stuff they should do. That's what's wrong with the world. Too many people blaming other people and events for their unfortunate circumstances; too many people telling themselves and others what they should and should not be doing.

"It's not Terry's fault. But it is his responsibility. This is a great opportunity for Terry to remember how to create real business. Business that is sustainable and long-term. This client is giving him a great chance to learn how to respond when things aren't perfect.

"We all know that things go wrong in life. The client will know that too. What they'll want to see is that this company is willing to engage in the process to make things better. Terry at the moment is doing the classic 'head-in-the-sand' posture. And when you do that all people see is what an ass you are—or have."

Brenda let out an uncontrollable laugh at the thought of Terry with his head in the sand and his rear end in the air.

"The important point here is that at some point Terry has got to learn to take responsibility for his actions. From what you said earlier, he clearly knows how to do that, he just needs reminding. As does this whole company from the top down. That can only happen if people like you, who are ultimately trusted and, believe it or not, vital to the company's continued survival, have the courage to state your own boundaries.

"By letting Terry get away with this type of thing, you are contributing to the company's poor performance. What seems like an act of kindness to you, is in real terms disempowering for you and Terry and Straight-Talking Finance Ltd."

Brenda was feeling uncomfortable again. "Oh

great, so it's my fault now is it that the company's going pear-shaped?"

The Coach remained clear and calm. "Brenda, it's not about blame, remember? It's about choice. It's about response-ability. How you respond to things. Your responsibility is to yourself. Start being kind to yourself and people will start being kind to you. Start letting people know who Brenda really is and you'll find out even more about those people. Start respecting yourself and you will be respected. *But make yourself good at dealing with people's shit and that's precisely what they'll keep giving you to deal with.*'

Brenda ran her hand back across her head. What the Coach was saying made perfect sense. She didn't like it, but it did make sense. She had never really thought about how she could be doing anything but helping people when she lied for them; but now she could see that what she was doing was nothing more than helping to perpetuate a myth.

"So helping people doesn't necessarily mean doing exactly what they ask? Really helping someone might even mean landing them in the shit?" Brenda looked particularly concerned by this suggestion.

The Coach was quick on the up-take: "Absolutely, a) if it is reflective of your truth and b) if this means you're giving them the chance to take responsibility for their own actions. Anything which helps someone to avoid issues that they're going to have to learn to deal with some day is nothing more than a delaying tactic which always results in greater suffering along the way for all concerned." The Coach was not going to shift on this one. He was as clear as a bell and Brenda was really beginning to understand what he was on about.

"So how are you going to deal with it from here Brenda?" Brenda thought about the different choices that lay in front of her. She was just beginning to prepare an answer when there was a knock at the door of the meeting-room. Brenda felt her stomach suddenly drop when the door opened. It was her boss, James Duncan.

11

Brenda jumped guiltily to her feet and greeted the CEO. Why she should feel guilty wasn't clear; she assumed that by meeting with the Coach she was purely complying with the company's wishes after all.

James Duncan was a well-built, handsome man in his mid forties with swept back blond hair. Although not particularly tall, his straight back and upright manner made him appear bigger than he really was. He was always dressed immaculately— he never went in for any of the casual look so beloved by the American owners.

"Good morning." He fixed his eyes on Brenda. "A quick word Brenda?" He spoke clearly and with authority. Brenda followed him out into the main office. The Coach sat back in his chair and waited.

Brenda felt a mixture of nervousness at the unexpected appearance of her boss and calmness thanks to the renewed sense of identity that she had been beginning to get in touch with during her meeting.

"What's the problem James? I wasn't expecting you in until about 3.30pm."

"Thanks to that ridiculous late show last night, I forgot to take the disc that's got the Stones' PowerPoint on it. You haven't seen it have you? I'm buggered if I can remember where I left it."

Brenda strode confidently over to her desk, pulled out the top drawer and extracted a CD-ROM which she then placed in James's hand. He gave her a smile that made her feel ten feet tall. "Great find Brenda. Right I'm off. Can you just call Mather and tell him I'm on my way. I'll probably be a few minutes late." He was literally heading out of the door by now, but Brenda just managed to stop him.

"James why don't *you* call him from your mobile? I'm sure he'd much rather hear from you than from me. He is head of UK Business after all. He'll appreciate your honesty."

Duncan was not best pleased. "What?" But he was in too much of a hurry to argue. "Oh bloody hell, alright I'll call him." He paused momentarily and then said more quietly, "you're probably right anyway, you normally are." With that he flew out of the door, muttered a quiet "geez do I have to do everything round here?" to himself and then legged it down the stairs (a time-motion study had shown them that it was generally quicker than taking the lift when time was an issue).

Brenda uttered a quiet "Y-E-S" as she allowed herself to enjoy the feeling of strength that had just come up as a result of her trying out this honesty lark that the Coach had been going on about. She didn't have to make yet another apologetic phone call and her boss had acknowledged that this was the correct course of action.

She went back to tell the Coach what had happened.

But the White Room was empty.

12

James selected the number from his memory on the tiny mobile phone that his daughter had selected for him on a recent shopping expedition.

"Gary Mather please, it's James Duncan." James quickly caught his breath a minute waiting for Mather to come to the phone.

"Gary? James here. Look sorry about this but I'm running a few minutes late, probably won't be there for another 10 minutes. Just wanted to let you know."

The voice at the other end of the phone acknowledged the call. James continued.

"No problem at all Gary, hate keeping people waiting myself. And much prefer to tell you personally rather than getting some PA to carry the can. See you in a minute."

James was clearly surprised by the positive response he got on the phone. He smiled. *"Clever girl that Brenda"* he thought to himself.

13

Serena Miller was still in a state of shock. It had been about an hour or so since her husband had called to say that he was going to be home for the evening and could they have a meal together tonight, preferably with Kieran as well if he fancied it. *"If Kieran fancies it"*. Even his language had been different from normal.

She had been sitting wondering about all the possible reasons why Julian would suddenly want to do such a thing. The only possible cause that she could come up with was that he had been fired.

The thing was though he hadn't sounded upset. If anything he had sounded quite happy. Happier than she had heard him in a long time. And the way that he had suggested Kieran join them if he wanted to was a million miles away from his normal controlling nature.

She had to know more and she had to know *now*. She reached for the phone. Brenda's familiar voice welcomed her:

"Hi Brenda, it's Serena. Can I have a quick word with Julian?" Serena tapped her fingers on the side of the breakfast bar whilst she waited for Julian to answer.

"Oh, hi darling. Look, tonight, no, no it's not a problem. It's just that, well it seems so unusual and I was worried that maybe something bad had happened ... nothing bad? Nothing bad at all? Oh, so you haven't lost your job or anything?" She had barely dared to ask up to now but his tone gave her more confidence.

"Okay darling, well thank you. Yes I'll sort out something special to eat and I'll see you about 6.30. Love you too."

"How totally weird" thought Serena as she opened up Delia's Summer Collection. *"Nice, but weird..."*

14

Down in the courtyard that the office informally shared with various other city workers and errant tourists off the beaten track, Terry Johnson was lighting up. He noticed his hand shaking a little as he struck the match. Well, it had been a stressful morning not to mention a heavy night. He reasoned with himself that he had good reason to have a shaky hand.

He was reminding himself how he must not let his guard drop. *"Don't let anyone know you're feeling vulnerable"* he kept repeating to himself. Least of all Brenda. He knew full well that she was the channel for every bit of information going round the office; letting her know that he was shit scared of failing to hit his targets again (for the second quarter in a row) would be the equivalent of admitting failure. And as for the family split, well you could forget that. If news got out about that they'd soon put two and two together to make five and conclude that the reason for his ailing performance was down to personal problems. They'd have him out of there in no time flat. No, much better not to tell anyone, including Brenda, anything.

It sounded easy. Just don't tell anyone anything. But it was beginning to drive him crazy. There was a part of him that was desperate to share his story with someone at work. It was getting to the stage where it wouldn't really have mattered who. Brenda appeared in his train of thought again. He liked her and at some other level he sensed he really could trust her. And there was a part of him that hated giving her his crap to deal with all the time. Somehow though that was precisely what he was expected to do. But expected by whom? And who wrote this goddamn book of business expectations and behaviour anyway?

The selling he loved. Always had. Natural born salesman he'd always been told. "You could sell cheese to a bloody dairy farm" his dad had said to him. His dad had loved cheese. Smelly cheese. Really stinky stuff like gorgonzola and stilton.

He missed his dad. God, how he missed him. He had died two years previously. Totally unexpected. Just dropped dead in his allotment. Nice way to go, he loved his allotment. But Terry still hadn't come to terms with it. He knew he hadn't. He missed him so badly sometimes he wanted to cry. But hey he couldn't do that, he was a bloke.

"I miss my father too Terry." Terry looked to his left side where an unfamiliar voice had interrupted his train of thought.

"How the ..." but before Terry could go on to express his confusion at how this stranger had known what he was thinking, the man carried on speaking.

"And there's no simple solution to it either. I mean this is one of those problems you definitely can't fix. Your dad, my dad, all the millions of ex-dads all over the universe, they're just not going to be there ever again to make it alright. To make us feel safe. It's a bummer, but that's how it is. It'd be good though wouldn't it? I mean, just sometimes to have someone else take responsibility for all this stuff sometimes?"

The stranger engaged Terry in such a way that he felt powerless to resist the dialogue. "Huh. My dad take responsibility for anything. Now there's a joke. He wouldn't take responsibility for his farting let alone anything bigger." Terry kicked in the direction of a pigeon that had come foolishly close to his right foot.

The stranger spoke again. "That must have been hard. Having a dad I mean that didn't take responsibility for things."

Terry responded coldly "I learnt to deal with it. I remember once, he was a gambler you see my dad, it was my birthday and he spent all my birthday money down the dogs at Hackney Stadium. My mum went ballistic the night before my birthday and I heard them having the most terrible row. I was probably about 10 or so. All he kept saying was 'it wasn't my fault, it wasn't my fault'. I think he was crying too."

The stranger spoke gently to Terry. "That must have been hard to take at that age. What do you think you learnt from it Terry?"

By now, Terry was so immersed in his story that he had completely forgotten the fact that he didn't even know who this bloke was.

"What did I learn from it? What did *I* learn from it? Well I guess I'd never really thought I'd learnt anything from it. But I suppose, well I learnt not to trust my dad ever again. I learnt that the world isn't always fair and that if something goes wrong it's not my fault…"

"And do you still think that is true? Is life unfair? When things go wrong is it really somebody else's fault always? Does it empower you to think that you can always blame someone else if things don't work out?" The stranger picked up the tempo.

Terry looked thoughtful. "Whoa, hold on there. That's a lot of questions. But, yes, life is unfair sometimes. And yes it does help me to feel I can blame someone else for a cock-up. It helps me to stop feeling so guilty."

The mystery man replied calmly. "But Terry, what does that blame do for the other person? Does it make them feel good?"

"Well, that's their look-out. If they screw up, they have to carry the can. It's all about responsibility."

The stranger smiled. His thoughts entirely. "Yes Terry, it is all about responsibility. But I think you're missing something really important here. You're passing responsibility to others for the shit when it happens, but what responsibility are you taking yourself for allowing it to enter your life in the first place? When you engage in something that involves others surely you all have to take equal responsibility for the success or failure of that project?"

Terry did not like the way this conversation was going. He was feeling decidedly uncomfortable and got to his feet to leave, suddenly remembering that he had no idea who this man was with whom he was engaged in 'meaningful' conversation.

"Look, this has been great but I have to go…"

The stranger didn't get up. He just reached out his hand to Terry and as they shook he looked him clearly in the eyes. Terry turned awkwardly to leave at which point the stranger called after him and asked, "Just tell me one thing Terry. How are you doing with hitting your targets?"

Terry stopped dead in his tracks.

15

"Look, who the hell are you? And how do you know all this about me? What do you know about my targets?" Terry was showing clear signs of agitation. The stranger didn't seem flustered.

"Let's just say it's my business to know about these things Terry. Now, these targets of yours, wouldn't you like to be hitting them every quarter?"

The stranger had Terry's attention once again. There was nothing like the thought of hitting targets to get Terry engaged.

"Like it? Like it? D-u-r-r! Of course I'd like it." Terry sat down again, wanting to know whether this carrot that he felt was being dangled was for real or not.

"Well, it's entirely possible Terry. But maybe

the way to start achieving it is not in ways that you're thinking about right now. Tell me. What's your view of the market right now?"

Terry didn't stop to consider his words. "Tough. Very, very tough. We've had a shit year in the UK, but then so has the global company. And whilst our numbers here are down, they're no worse than any of the overseas teams. The market's tough and it's going to stay that way for quite a while it looks like."

The stranger looked on and smiled. "Terry, we're going to have do something about your language." Terry looked confused, trying to remember whether he had just said something offensive.

"No, it's not your swearing I'm talking about Terry. It's the way you're viewing how the market is going to be. It's how you're talking about what you're expecting to happen. You want to start getting better results? Well we've got to help you to start expecting them first."

Terry looked at the stranger quizzically. "You're

not going to try to tell me that the reason I'm failing to close is because of the way I'm talking about the state of the market?"

"Well put it this way Terry, I don't think your negative assessment of the market is helping you. You see I've got some pretty mad theories about life. Ideas which spring from wisdom which has been passed down through the ages. One of those theories is that whatever you believe you are going to experience, you almost certainly will." The stranger was getting into his stride as Terry listened closely.

"Remind yourself over and over again of how tough the market is for example, and I will guarantee you that you will experience a tough market. Why? Because that is what you are expecting to experience. It's no more complicated than that. Is every single person experiencing a tough market right now? No, of course not. Some are experiencing an easy market, a market where they can clean up. And if *anyone at all* is experiencing it as an easy market then that easy market must exist. And perhaps these people, few as they may be, are not expecting the market to be tough.

"Terry, you've bought into the myth that the market-place and the media want you to believe. But that does not mean it has to be your truth. And when we look at your truth we see that in this 'tough' market, you have out-performed every other European salesman and that the UK is still at the top of the European list in the last twelve months. Tell me, how much business have you closed in the last 12 months?"

Terry answered quietly. "£1.3 million. But I did it all in the first quarter. And my target for the year is £2 million which recently has seemed like a million miles away."

The stranger was smiling again. "So let me get this right. In this so-called 'tough' market of yours you have closed over a million pounds worth of business—correct?"

Terry nodded.

"Terry, when was the last time you ever closed deals worth £1.3 million pounds in your first quarter?"

Terry replied quickly." Never."

The stranger continued. "Never. So you could say in fact that this year to date has been your best year ever?"

Terry started to say something but the words never quite came out. Instead he just nodded his head. He was beginning to think at the same time.

"So Terry, history is telling us that you are having your best year ever, and yet your failure to hit your latest targets and your fear of not hitting your annual target are combining to tell you that it's a tough market." The stranger paused for a minute allowing Terry time to reflect on this. He then picked up his thread again.

"Tell me Terry, what approach are you taking with your potential champions and new business at the moment?"

Terry thought about this before answering. "Well I've started to be quite a bit more aggressive. I'm making hundreds of calls to new leads every week to try to widen my net. The CEO says it's all about numbers and he wants me getting as many appointments as possible in my diary. He doesn't want to see me at my desk until a shed-load of new business is closed. I'm seeing whoever will see me. It's a sort of *'throw enough mud against the wall and see if some of it sticks'* philosophy."

As he was speaking, Terry realised he was quite angry about this new direction that his selling had taken.

"And is this how you have always sold things Terry?"

Terry took a deep breath. He felt relieved just to be talking about this stuff at last. He'd been bottling it up for ages. "No, this isn't me. Believe it or not my natural approach is much more instinctive. Softly softly catchee monkey sort of thing. I always want to get the bigger deals, and I know to get them I have to spend a while building up a relationship with my champion. So this last few months of going purely after numbers has been totally alien to me."

"And coincidentally in that time you haven't closed one deal?"

"Well, no, now that you come to mention it I haven't. Not one."

There was a silence as Terry reflected on this observation.

The stranger felt no desire to hurry Terry out of his thoughts. He let what was at least a couple of minutes go by before speaking again.

"And one more thing Terry. Your targets for this year, they're based on what, a percentage increase from achievements last year right? And you will have agreed to them yes?"

Terry nodded his head again, still quiet in thought.

"And I bet, being you, you didn't want to demonstrate any form of weakness by asking for the targets to be reduced. Am I right again?"

"Yes, you're right again."

"Well, bearing in mind the fact that this year's market is different from last year's, is it also possible that the bar was set unrealistically high for your targets this year?"

Terry was pensive. He looked across the

courtyard at a mass of pigeons that were fighting over some tiny crumbs that had just been thrown there by a woman having a sandwich on a nearby bench.

"Yes, that's entirely possible. I get carried away when they talk me up, tell me how well I could do next year, how much I could earn etcetera etcetera. And I fall for it. Goddam it I fall for it. And that's when I fall into panic and I guess that gets noticed by Duncan who then starts giving me these absurd methods for getting more leads. When what I really need and want to do is to concentrate on consolidating the relationships I've already got because that's where all my business has always come from. People who know me and who trust me."

Terry was feeling lighter by the minute as he recognised who he really was as a salesman. No wonder he'd been feeling terrible and performing crap. He was using methods totally alien to his nature. He looked at the man beside him and this time, for the first time, he really looked into his eyes. He felt like he had shared more with this stranger

91

than he had with anyone in the company in the whole four years he had been there. And he also knew that he trusted this man entirely.

"So now what do I do?" Terry asked in a way which suggested he really wanted an answer.

The stranger stood up. "Oh, that's easy Terry. Just watch the birdies."

Terry turned his attention over to the birds who were making quite a noise and were now engaged in a pretty aggressive battle in their fight for the woman's crumbs. Terry felt the stranger tap him on the arm. He was asking him to look at a point under a bench about five feet away from the struggling birds.

There was the same woman sitting on the bench just finishing her sandwich and underneath the bench sat one very calm pigeon. After a couple of minutes the woman finished her drink, picked up her things, and left a couple of large crusts on the bench. The relaxed bird waited until she had gone, then jumped up onto the bench and flew off with both crusts in its mouth. The other birds, ignorant of this easy feast, were left still fighting over their paltry scraps.

Terry was transfixed. The analogy was perfect. He was choosing to engage in the same struggle as everyone else instead of reminding himself of his ability to stand back and be selective. And that is where it had all started going wrong. Once the panic of 'there's no business out there' had started to establish itself he had just bought into the myth of it along with everyone else. But this market was the same one in which he had had his best ever quarter, it was all a matter of perspective.

He kept his eyes fixed firmly on the fighting birds. "So what you're saying is I should be seeing this as an easy market. A market full of opportunities. A market where I can shine. A market where I can continue to establish my relationships and play the waiting game in the knowledge that my patience will lead me to the richest pickings?"

But no-one heard these last few words other than himself. The stranger had gone.

16

François sat at his desk staring at the latest email from the Webber group IT head. It was another headache. Problems with currency calculations in the software solution provided by Straight-Talking had left Webber facing a loss of over 20,000 euros in just one month. Not vast sums admittedly in comparison to the numbers being generated, but enough to be getting Webber's top brass involved.

François was desperate to keep this from Duncan but he wasn't sure how he was going to manage it this time. He'd already avoided letting him know there had been a problem over the last three weeks. A problem which had not been dealt with properly because Dima, the techie in charge of the account, was away and there was still no system in place for bringing deputising team members up to speed.

Crazy really. Here they were a company selling software solutions to financial institutions. And yet the software was not completely thought out and the tech team, whose job was to innovate, were constantly finding themselves fire-fighting. Dealing with problems that a lack of time and lack of budget had created in the first place. It was all so horribly short-term.

Neither had it escaped his notice that the new Phillips' deal was already showing signs of problems. He'd heard Brenda's shout earlier that morning and had been copied in on a couple of emails.

Now that really could develop into something disastrous for François, since he had been the one to overrule Matt who had said the software was not ready to handle the work that Phillips were looking for. François knew damn well that sooner or later the software would come up short but he was buggered if he was going to let some young smartarse like Matt start to call the shots, so he'd approved the deal in spite of himself. Still, that problem would still take a few weeks to really show itself by which time he hoped that one of the technical team would have come up with a solution.

The tech team all worked from the same large, round table. Their computers all backed on to each others meaning that they could not see the person sitting opposite unless they stood up or walked round the table. This had resulted in an extraordinary phenomenon. Virtually all their communication took place via email.

Matt and François sat at opposite sides of this table. François had never liked Matt, he found him too clever by half. As a result he had sought ways of undermining Matt's position, something which had been fairly easy to do as head of IT. Matt had already been officially warned twice, one more time and he'd be out. For François that day couldn't come a moment too soon.

His thoughts snapped back to the moment. Another email had just arrived, he had been cc'd on an email sent by Webber's head of sales to Terry. This thing was going higher and it was going higher quick. François was thrown into panic. What the fuck to do now? Even though he was the head of IT he knew his own limitations. He was a Steady Eddie, a good basic knowledge and understanding but not a man with innovative solutions to help solve problems. Quite honestly, François was still surprised himself that he'd ended up in charge of IT.

Dima could have done something. Probably. But he was away. That only left Matt. Matt. That little 'sh-e-e-t' as François had often silently thought of him. He leaned back. He could see Matt's feet doing the relentless tapping on the floor that they always did. Asking Matt for help was about as high up on François's list of most hated things as anything could be. He stared back at his screen. The email sat there motionless, pumping out the same message of fear second upon second.

François thought about the situation for a few more seconds and then decided on a course of action.

He got up and headed for the sandwich shop.

17

The Coach came out of the lift just as a flustered looking François was heading into it. The Coach said a polite 'Hi' to him and received a barely audible grunt in return. François pressed the ground floor button and waited for the doors to shut.

The Coach paused for a few seconds outside the door to the office, waiting to see whether François would re-appear. But then he heard the lift doors shut and the lift descending. François wasn't ready. Yet.

18

It was 11.45 am. As the Coach entered, Brenda beamed a smile at him that told him that she was already beginning to enjoy her new found confidence.

"It worked with James. Your suggestion it worked, like a charm. I suggested to him that he make his own phone call to apologise for being late and after a moment's consideration he agreed. Awesome. Totally awesome." Brenda was ecstatic. Ecstatic. Over such a simple thing. But then that was the key to the Coach's work. It always was simple. It had to be. Otherwise no-one would ever be able to do it or make it last.

"That's great Brenda, well done. How did that feel?" The Coach really wanted to know.

"Like I said. Awesome. I just felt so much—so much lighter I guess. Like I wasn't taking on his stuff. And the funny thing was, he didn't seem to mind that much."

"Wonderful Brenda. That's just the beginning." The Coach winked at her. "Is the White Room still available?"

Brenda checked down her schedule. "No Coach, sorry but there's a twelve o'clock coming in. The conference room is free though—do you want to go in there?"

Brenda stood up and ushered the Coach over to the larger room. He had a quick look. The room was bigger, less personal and a bit harsher somehow than the more intimate White Room.

"I'll give it a try Brenda, thanks. Can I get another glass of water?"

Brenda replied instantly "I'll get one for you, just you wait in there."

"Brenda listen to my language. I said can *I* get another glass of water? Your phone is ringing, you've got plenty to do. You don't need to be my, or anybody else's mother. I am a grown man and quite capable of filling up my own water glass. It's a very polite offer you made but please see to your own things." The Coach was firm and clear. Brenda at first felt a tang of rejection, but by the time she had answered the phone she had moved on.

The Coach went and filled his glass and returned to the conference room. He sat down and took a deep breath, contemplating his morning so far. He allowed his thoughts to settle as they often did on one particular incident or conversation, and then watched as they played around with the information of the last three hours. He was in no hurry to see anybody, choosing instead to sit in quiet and reflective contemplation.

He was brought out of his reverie by the sound of Terry's voice. He was in conversation with a French sounding man. The Coach assumed this must be François. There was clearly tension in their voices.

"Terry we have to talk about the Webber deal. They're all over us, you've got an email from Hodges waiting for you on the machine." François was talking at the same time as taking the wrapper off a chocolate bar from which he now bit off a large piece.

"Bollocks. Brenda, the White Room, is it free?" Terry looked over to Brenda who was busy writing at her desk.

"There's a 12 o'clock about to start in there I'm afraid Terry. And the confe..." but before Brenda could finish, Terry and François had already gone through the half open door of the conference room.

Terry stopped in his tracks when he saw the stranger he had been talking to in the courtyard sitting in one of the chairs.

19

"Good morning Terry—again." The Coach smiled as Terry looked totally confused.

"But, what are you..." and then he remembered he had François alongside him and not wanting to give away anything from his previous conversation with this stranger, he quickly regained his composure.

"Sorry, is this room taken?"

The Coach replied clearly. "It is now. Sit down Gentlemen. I'm the Coach, I'm here to help you with your little problem."

"You mean you work for Straight-Talking?" Terry looked even more concerned thinking back to how honest he had been during his meeting in the square with this enigmatic man.

"In a manner of speaking, yes I suppose you could say that Terry. My business is change. Positive, sustainable, innovative change. Now do you guys want help with this particular problem of yours or do you want to sort it out for yourselves?"

François had remained silent throughout this brief exchange. He now looked to Terry for leadership.

"Can we just have a chat between ourselves a minute?" Terry inquired of the Coach.

"Sure, take as long as you want. This will only work if you both want to do it." The Coach stayed resolutely in his chair and the two men went back out into the corridor, pulled the door to and discussed this unexpected turn of events.

"Who the crap is that?" whispered François as soon as they were out of the room.

Brenda overheard François's question and couldn't help answering before Terry had a chance to open his mouth which was just as well because Terry didn't really know.

"Him? He's the Coach. The Americans sent him. He's a business coach and let me tell you he is totally awesome. In the space of a few minutes this morning he has taught me how to handle Duncan with something and it totally worked.

And from what I've seen of the looks on the faces of Shanti, Julian and Matt when they've come out of meetings with him, I'd say he's probably already helped them too. If he's giving you a chance to meet, grab it with both hands. Oops, sorry Terry, did I interrupt?" Just at that moment one of the phones went again and Brenda returned to her work.

Terry looked at François. He hadn't said anything. François's question had been answered and he was already heading back into the conference room.

20

"Come in François". The Coach welcomed the head of IT into the room and beckoned to him to sit down. François looked behind him for Terry but found that he was alone. His initial bravado waned. He went back out to find Terry, only to discover that the phone call Brenda had taken must have been for Terry as he was now engaged in an animated conversation at his desk.

François thought about what to do. He found his heart racing a little faster than normal. He didn't like the idea of going in to talk to this coach guy alone. What if he started probing him about his technical nous or why he had been so bullish in approving the Phillips' deal.

He quickly returned to his desk and sat down at his keyboard. He pulled up his Outlook Express programme and emailed Brenda. "Hi B, had to attend to urgent problem re Webber solution. Please tell Coach I can't meet."

François heaved a sigh of relief and returned to the familiar territory of his comfort zone. Time would sort it. The problems would get solved. Just keep your head down if the bullets start flying around the place.

He looked at his inbox. Five more emails were waiting for him. In amongst the normal suspects, François's attention was drawn to one in particular which made his heart beat even faster than when he had been about to see the Coach. It had just been sent by Terry and was entitled "Phillips—shit and fan."

Terry's phone call had indeed been an urgent one. His Phillips' champion had finally got hold of him. One of the tech team at Phillips had flagged up a potentially serious problem with the software solution. A problem which could put Straight-Talking in breach of contract and result in the whole deal being blown. François knew that it wouldn't only be his job on the line if this one fell through.

He looked over towards Terry's desk. Terry was standing up, waiting for the Frenchman's reaction to the email. Terry pointed towards the conference room, where the Coach still sat patiently waiting for his next challenge.

François and Terry met outside and without saying a word to each other entered the room.

"Hello again Gentlemen. Have a seat."

The calmness in the Coach's voice immediately put the two men more at ease.

"So, who wants to tell me what the problem is with you two?"

François's body language was that of someone who didn't entirely trust the person he was sitting opposite. Arms were folded, legs crossed. He wasn't going to give anything away easily.

Terry was less apprehensive.

"Well, to put it quite simply because I don't know how technical you are, we have a glitch with our portfolio solution. Nothing that can't be fixed, but it's causing a little inconvenience right now."

Both Terry and François were pleased at the way in which Terry had managed to play the problem down.

This was meat and potatoes to the Coach. "So this software problem can be fixed is that right François?"

"Er, yes, I'm sure it can be. Yeah it happens all the time this sort of thing."

François continued to dig the hole that Terry had started.

The Coach continued "So guys, what are you doing in here if all you've got is a software problem that you can fix. Wouldn't you be better off out there fixing it?"

There was a silence that seemed to last for an eternity. Terry found himself not knowing what to say. François was totally perplexed and was making ready to go. His automatic response to any situation where he found himself without an answer was to escape as quickly as possible.

"Unless of course..." continued the Coach "...you haven't got an answer to it right now. Now then in that situation I could probably help you."

Terry and François looked at each other. François was terrified of anyone finding out what he didn't know, that he wasn't really a technical genius after all. Terry was terrified of dropping his guard again to reveal the vulnerable, insecure man that lay beneath this smooth, polished exterior.

"Okay mate, I'm going to stay. Although I'm not convinced there's anything you can do about this one—it's a technical problem we've got here." Terry looked across at François who was standing by the door. "François we're already fucked, what have we got to lose?"

François nodded his head in partial agreement and sat down again. The Coach rubbed his hands together like someone who had just had some good news.

"Okay guys, let's have some fun…"

21

James Duncan emerged from the meeting with Gary Mather with his tail between his legs. Who the hell did Mather think he was, talking about the lack of integrity he sensed at Straight-Talking? And how dare he suggest that the UK company seemed to be implementing a short-term 'anything-for-a-quick-buck' policy.

And why, oh why, would Stones have asked them to pitch for the business in the first place if they thought Straight-Talking were so irresponsible? And what about that comment stating his disappointment that Terry wasn't involved in the final presentation? What was all that about?

As he walked down the street back towards the office he became angrier and angrier. He started to list the people in his mind who had screwed this presentation up for him. Top of his list was Terry. What on earth was he doing claiming that this deal was "as good as closed"? Hadn't he realised that they hadn't even got out of the starting blocks?

Next to get it would be the tech team. François was the IT head so that's where Duncan would start. Mather had pointed out one major flaw in the software solution. Duncan had felt his stomach tighten up when this had been mentioned during the meeting—he knew that it was the same software solution that they had already successfully sold to Phillips and Webber and were now implementing. Mind you, there had been no come-back there yet. Maybe Mather's tech team had got it wrong.

By the time he had reached the doors of the building he had built up a good head of steam. The lift doors opened and he prepared himself for what was becoming an almost weekly display of fireworks. It was happening so often now that it seemed totally natural. And it certainly seemed to have the desired effect of motivating his team into action each time.

22

Brenda could tell by how James Duncan entered through the single glass door whether he was in one of his moods or not. The office could become a changed environment within seconds, such was the effect of the man. No-one could doubt he had charisma. Everyone wanted to be liked by him, everyone wanted to be approved of by him so if he was in a black space it impacted heavily on the whole office.

On his way past Brenda to the White Room he commanded her to send in Terry first and then François.

"But James…" Brenda protested but it was too late. Duncan had stormed into the room and burst in upon a meeting that Shanti was having with the European head of media.

111

Duncan didn't say a word. He just stormed out again and shut the door. Shanti felt her whole body tense up. Tight stomach, a head that had instantly started throbbing, she even felt her breathing change dramatically to sharp, short breaths. Normally these symptoms would lead to a major migraine and at least a day off work. Was this what the Coach was talking about when he connected her failing health to the lack of happiness and excess of stress in her working environment? She'd never made such a clear connection before but now that she thought about it, it seemed so clear.

God she was fed up with these games that James played. When something was up with him he always made sure everyone knew about it. In those moments he often reminded her of Dudley Dursley from the Harry Potter books that she loved so much.

Shanti tried to focus back on the job in hand. But it was no good. It was like a stream of intelligence had just been released throughout her body which was screaming for her to get out of there. She thought about some of the things the Coach had said and excused herself from the meeting for five minutes. She slipped out of the front door and went to seek the sanctuary of the square and some fresh air.

Back in the office, Duncan looked in at the conference room. Through the thin pane of frosted glass beside the door he just could make out three outlines and could discern the tone of François's voice. He turned back to Brenda.

"How long is François going to be? And who's he in with?"

Brenda couldn't help feeling that something interesting could be about to happen here. What would the Coach make of this situation?

"Well he's in there with Terry, they went in about 15 minutes ago. They're both with the Coach."

Duncan pondered for a few seconds. "Okay well I want to see Terry the second he's finished, and François after that. Tell them to cancel whatever appointments they've got for early this afternoon. We've got some serious shit to sort out."

He started over for his desk. And then he paused, thought and returned to Brenda's desk. This

113

time he spoke a little more quietly.

"They're in with *who?*"

Brenda was silent. From the look on Duncan's face it was clear that he had never heard of the Coach.

23

"François, what's the best thing that could happen to you at work this week?" The Coach was now in his element, grappling with a problem that, according to the two people sitting opposite him, had no solution.

François responded in his typical sardonic French way. "I get given a 25% pay rise and we get a fresh coffee dispenser in the office?"

The Frenchman laughed, Terry smiled as did the Coach.

"Okay François, let's try that again. In relation to your current situation and problems, what's the best thing that could happen at work this week?" The Coach remained firm and patient. François reconsidered.

"Well the best thing that could happen is..." he hesitated. He was clearly struggling with the degree of honesty that the Coach seemed effortlessly to be drawing out of him.

"I suppose the best thing would be that we sort out a solution to this software problem on the different accounts." François felt his body relax a little just at the acknowledgement of this truth.

The Coach turned to Terry. "Terry, what about you? What would be the best thing that could happen to you this week at work?"

"I don't have to spend any time trying to smooth over problems relating to deals we've already closed and get on with what I love. Chasing new business." Just the thought of this brought a sense of relief to Terry's stomach. He could sense a very real physical and mental lightening.

The Coach returned his attention to François. "François you said the best thing that could happen this week would be for a solution to be sorted on the software. My next question is this. Is there anything more you can do right now to help make that happen?"

François was quiet. This was the big one. He knew he could do nothing. This was what he relied on Dima and Matt for—solutions. But he was the boss and he hated the thought of anyone knowing that he couldn't do everything, that members of his team had more technical know-how than him. He fidgeted uncomfortably in his chair.

" I, er, I, I guess I need the time to sit down and study the software in detail and see where the glitches are." Even Terry could tell that François was holding back.

"Is that the truth François?" asked the Coach without hesitation. "Look, no one is judging you here and there is no 'right' answer. There is only truth. I would suggest to you both that the miracle that it seems you guys currently need can only happen when you can really own what's going on.

So I ask you again. Is there anything *you* can do right now to start correcting the software problem?"

"I suppose I need to explain the problem to Dima and get his feedback. But he's away until next week so that leaves me totally fucked right now."

116

François's ego was clearly having a big fight at this public acknowledgement of needing somebody else's help.

The Coach concentrated his look on François again. "François, is there anyone else who could maybe give you some ideas as to how to fix this? Is Dima definitely the only one with the know-how?"

François could feel himself welling up with anger at where the Coach was leading him. Yes Matt could probably help him, but dammit that would show Matt that he had power over him. The last thing François wanted was that little upstart having a chance to demonstrate he was more technically gifted than he was. He'd never forgotten that dream he had had months ago where he was in a Land-Rover driving around the countryside waiting for instructions to pick up Matt who was way above him in a hot air balloon. He hated the idea of Matt having any control over him at all.

He looked back at the Coach. "No, there is no-one else who can help." The Coach knew this was untrue, but he also knew that the miracles only happen when the individual concerned comes up with the answers. This was such a familiar block and he knew in that instant that François was resistant to change. His ego was getting in the way. His unwillingness to demonstrate humility by asking for Matt's help was indicative of a resistance that would inevitably result in him experiencing further similar negative situations in the future. A good leader recognises the experts in his team whatever their standing and makes the most of their skills. François was clearly too threatened and insecure to be seen asking for help from a junior.

The Coach observed in himself a slight sense of sadness that much of the smoothness he had experienced so far today had hit a block with François. But it also reassured him in a way as to the authenticity of what he was doing. He had never yet been in an organisation where everyone had been willing to change their limited views immediately and François's intransigence affirmed this historical pattern. He also knew he had to take François as far as he could.

"Okay François another question. Who are the people hassling you over these problems?"

François answered this question more easily. "Terry, because he's starting to get it from the clients he's sold to. And I guess Duncan will be after me as soon as he finds out."

"Okay, well presumably Terry is aware of the problems to some extent. Right Terry?" Terry nodded his head. This time the Coach addressed Terry. "Terry is there any more you'd like to know from François right now about this situation?"

François shuffled again in his seat. Terry thought about the question and answered. "Yes, I'd like to know if I can tell clients when we can expect to sort the problems."

François wasn't happy. Terry knew he didn't have the answer to that one. So did the Coach, who offered François a clue to help him provide an answer.

"François am I right in thinking that you can't do anything about this until Dima returns next Monday?" François nodded in agreement. The Coach continued, aware that François was still refusing to acknowledge Matt's potential input.

"And am I also right in thinking that no-one else can do anything to help whilst Dima is away?" François nodded again. "So François you can give Terry some timings. You can say that you are aware of the situation and that you'll throw everything you can at this when Dima returns on Monday. Isn't that right?"

François nodded rather pathetically in agreement. The Coach carried on. "François speak it. Put it in your own words. It's okay not to have all the answers. Come from your truth and you'll only ever get great stuff back."

François hesitated before opening his mouth. "Okay Terry, I'm aware of the problem with the software. There's nothing I can do before Monday when Dima returns so there's no point in hassling me between now and then." François felt like he was back at school in drama class reading a script for the first time.

The Coach could feel the strong resistance that

François felt in owning even this. He wondered what else must have been going on inside this proud man that he couldn't even allow himself to consider engaging Matt's help. François wasn't ready for change. He was obviously going to need a bigger crisis than this to kick him out of ego. The Coach acknowledged and accepted this answer.

"Thanks François. Now you can give yourself permission not to spend any more time worrying about how to fix this problem this week. Anyone asks you about it you have your answer fully prepared: 'I'm aware of the problem and am waiting the return of one of my tech team on Monday to start fixing it.' Agreed?"

François shuffled again. "Agreed."

"Great" said the Coach "You can now get back to your other work. It's been interesting meeting with you." The Coach was about to usher François out of the room when there was a knock at the door.

The Coach responded very calmly. "Come in."

The powerful figure of James Duncan entered the room. He wasn't happy.

24

Julian emerged from the DVD rental shop with a treasured copy of "Bill and Ted's Excellent Adventure", one of his son's favourite films and one both he and Serena had found surprisingly amusing. There was something about those Wyld Stallyns that a part of Julian yearned to be like.

He pulled a small piece of paper out of his pocket. On it Brenda had scrawled a sketchy map to help him find the florist. God, all these years working here and he'd never been to the flower shop. Never taken her back any flowers. What a jerk.

The directions were perfect. Of course. That's Brenda for you. He silently thanked her.

Entering the shop he was at once dazzled and freaked out by the array of colour that lay in front of him. He also felt embarrassed just like the first time he had when he'd bought condoms from a chemist.

His analytical mind was awash with the fear of making the wrong choice. How can you tell if the flowers are fresh? When would the buds open? Were the lilies any good? Were they the things that Serena had a problem with because of pollen dropping on to her clothes or was that something else? Should he get a mixed bunch of stuff in the hope that some of it would be right, or risk getting one bunch of the same thing and possibly screw up entirely.

A young female shop assistant asked him if he'd like any help. He felt himself blushing. How could buying a bunch of flowers pose such a challenge? He was starting to realise how screwed up and one dimensional his life had become. He wished he could be back in the safe environment of the DVD shop where he had felt far more in control.

He flashed back to the conversation he had had with the Coach earlier that morning. He'd identified in himself the problem he had in asking anyone for help. He reminded himself of his desire to change and plucked up every ounce of courage he could muster. "Mmm, well, yes I do think I need some help. I want some flowers for my wife and I haven't got the first idea what to get."

Julian became aware of a strange feeling flowing through him. He had totally dropped the façade of having all the answers and had allowed this young woman to see his ignorance. He felt liberated; free from the burden of expectation of having all the answers to all things.

The girl responded warmly. "Certainly sir. What is your wife's favourite colour?"

So logical, so simple. And a question Julian could answer. They spent the next ten minutes going round the shop choosing 'stems' and 'sprays' that blended together like a Dutch masterpiece. He thanked the girl not only for the flowers but also for his new education and left the shop carrying his beautiful gift.

He thought he'd feel embarrassed walking back down the road to the office. But he didn't. He felt excited. He walked along holding his flowers as proudly as athletes hold the Olympic Torch. He felt like he had felt the first time he'd sent a Valentine at school to Lucy Evans. A little bit scared, but mainly excited. Excited at the thought of the look on Serena's face when he would present the flowers to her tonight.

25

Matt sat at a counter in the local Starbucks staring out at the endless stream of City workers who hustled past each other on the pavement outside. He took a swig of Coke and another bite from his chicken salad ciabatta. He was thinking about his meeting with the Coach and the revolutionary ideas that had sprung from it.

He also thought about Susie and how she would react at the cancellation of their wedding. Whilst the thought of her reaction scared him a little, he also knew that he had to do it. The feeling hadn't weakened in the two hours or so since the meeting, it had strengthened.

It felt as if someone was cutting the shackles from around his legs and arms. He was beginning to feel strong and empowered. He found himself smiling at the thought of no longer being 'engaged'—probably of no longer having a girlfriend either since Susie wasn't likely to want to carry on seeing him if there was to be no marriage.

His thoughts wandered into business. The word 'freedom' kept on going round and round his head. He thought about what the Coach had drawn out of him; yes, the thought of proposing the customer log again to François felt good; but what felt really good hadn't even entered their conversation. What felt really good was of following that dream he had always had, the dream of setting up his own company.

And he knew he had the technical wizardry to do it. He had just never had the confidence or the self-belief. He wondered whether his meeting with the Coach might not have been the first step towards acquiring that confidence.

Matt finished up his meal and returned in a pretty happy state to the office. He got out of the lift and walked through the doors, determined to fix up a meeting with his fiancée and another with François.

As he passed by the door of the conference room he could see the figure of James Duncan standing in the doorway. Just by the way he was standing Matt could tell Duncan was angry. Besides which the office had that deathly hush about it that told him Duncan was on the warpath. Again. How tedious these black moods were becoming.

Matt kept his head down and headed straight for his desk where he started writing his first email. "Susie—we have to meet—7.30pm at my place." He typed it quickly and pressed send before he had a chance to reconsider. There. It was done. The ball of the rest of his life had just started rolling.

26

James Duncan didn't recognise the voice that answered when he knocked at the door of the conference room. It slightly threw him off his guard. He opened the door to see Terry sitting at the table and François looking like he was about to leave.

Sitting opposite was the man he had seen talking with Brenda earlier in the day. This must have been the mysterious coach that Brenda had mentioned.

He was just about to ask what this meeting was about when the Coach started talking. "Good afternoon James. I'm the Coach. You probably don't know about me. I'm here to help you guys sort out this shit you've got yourselves into."

The Coach had a way of using language that was entirely appropriate to the person he was addressing. Terry and François remained in the room, open-mouthed at the confident way in which the Coach was addressing their CEO. James stood there looking more than just a little disconcerted.

"Brenda's just told me about you 'Coach'. And what do you mean exactly by 'this shit'?"

The Coach knew James had taken the bait. He hadn't even questioned him on his identity or what he was doing there and who had sent him, he had just gone straight for the big one. Perfect.

"Well now James, should we talk about this with your colleagues here, or should you and me have a chat first?" The Coach held the CEO firmly in his gaze. James shuffled a bit on his feet before remembering what he was so riled up about.

"Look, Mr, er this is all very well but I have got an office to run here and I need to talk to Terry urgently about something so if you'll excuse us..." James was beginning to work up a head of steam and re-establish his authority within the room when the Coach brought him back to earth with a bang.

"James, may I ask? Would you be about to have a go at Terry because you've just lost a prospect? And did that prospect tell you that he felt Straight-Talking lacked integrity, that the company doesn't have the long-term well-being of the client in mind—that you're only really in it for a quick buck?"

James was silenced. He turned quite pale for a minute before pulling up the nearest chair and flopping into it. He looked shocked and felt confused. "How the hell do you know all this? Who are you?"

Terry and François had never seen this vulnerable side to their CEO before. For the first time

129

they found themselves feeling a degree of compassion for their boss.

The Coach turned to the two men. "Terry, François—will you give me a few minutes to talk to James? I'll give a shout when we need you back again."

Terry and François got up from their seats and left the room. The Coach looked across at James Duncan who had seemingly given up trying to hang onto his composure and was now visibly shaking.

"You and me have got some talking to do." The Coach started the meeting that would change the way that James Duncan did business for the rest of his life.

27

"Would you like some water, or a tea or something James?" The CEO shook his head. The Coach continued. "James to what percentage of its potential do you think this company is performing? I mean the

UK office."

It wasn't a question James Duncan had ever really considered before. Oh he knew all about targets and failure or success in achieving them, but he hadn't really thought about what the potential of the company was as a whole. He offered a weak response. "I don't know, maybe about seventy percent?"

The Coach allowed himself a smile. "Seventy percent? That would suggest to me that you're closing about two of every three deals you're going for and that current contracts are running at about seventy percent effectiveness. Is that about right?"

James knew this was way off mark. They had closed three in thirty deals over the last 18 months and were receiving an increasing number of complaints from existing clients.

"Well no I guess maybe it's a smaller number." The CEO was becoming more humble with every sentence even though he wasn't trying to. His resistance was weakening all the time.

The Coach suggested a different figure. "James

I reckon you're getting about ten percent effectiveness from everyone at the moment. Ten percent. Do you hear me?"

James reflected on this seemingly very negative assessment. He didn't offer any challenge to it, his silence confirming the Coach's judgement of the state of Straight-Talking's business.

"James have you any idea how this company would be performing if you were getting maybe fifty, sixty or even seventy percent more effectiveness from your teams?"

James thought for a moment. "Look, it's a tough market out there. We're not doing any worse than most of the others. This isn't our problem it's the market. It's tough out there. It's the same the world over."

It's tough out there. Hmm now where had the Coach heard those words before. James had trained Terry well. "Yes James maybe, but how differently might you be performing if you were getting more effective contributions from your staff and yourself? It can be done."

"I can't work these people any harder. I'm hard enough on them as it is. They'll be driven over the edge if I up the pressure any more." James spoke with an openness that impressed the Coach.

The Coach was delighted by this response. "No James, you're right. But this isn't about working harder. It's about working smarter. It's about running this business holistically…"

James butted in. "We are holistic. We must be one of the most holistic businesses in the City. Why this year alone I've taken the whole crew out on two corporate days to Brands Hatch and Stamford Bridge, we've done a team-building weekend in Wales and we've replaced the coke machine with a spring water dispenser."

The Coach let James reel off this list of so-called 'holistic' practices. How many times before had he heard the same sorts of things trotted off as meaning holistic. Nothing wrong with them in themselves, but holistic?

"James, we need to talk about what a holistic business really means. It's really very simple and a better understanding of it will help you to build the foundations upon which a sustainable, long-term business can be developed."

28

Following the disconcerting interruption from Duncan in the middle of her meeting, Shanti had managed to regain her composure following her five minutes 'time-out' down in the square. She returned feeling refreshed and calmer than she had felt in a long while at work.

She had noticed how her body had started to relax again as she had removed herself from the stress of the office and was really beginning to believe in the Coach's assertion that physical imbalances can be linked to emotional stress. When she returned to the meeting she experienced one of the most exciting sessions that she had ever had with her European Media head.

Lars Sorensen was nothing if not conservative,

and yet Shanti had managed to convince him to do a joint presentation with her where they would suggest a totally new lay-out and approach to the somewhat stodgy in-house monthly newsletter. Shanti had talked about incorporating personal stories to bring more heart into the business. Much to her surprise Lars had become quite animated and positive about the whole idea.

There would be employee profiles focusing on the things that employees like to do outside the business as well as some of their more interesting ideas for helping the business to change. There would be more photos and a new satirical column to bring some humour into the serious approach that presently held sway.

They would seek to change the lay-out so that it looked like something you could have a quick flick through without thinking that all you would be staring at would be figures. Oh the figures would still be there, but they'd be intermingling with a more personal, open-hearted approach.

Shanti really believed this would transform it

into a vehicle that could unite the European branches of the company far more than the annual knees-up and conference that currently shouldered the burden for pulling together the disparate factions of the company.

What Shanti didn't know is what an impact this conversation had had on Lars. He felt incredibly uplifted and inspired by Shanti's ideas. He had long felt that he was going through the motions in his role at STF and had been becoming more and more depressed by the monotony of trying to make numbers sound interesting.

His background was strictly accounting, but his strong English had made him the natural candidate for communications work within the company and when the role became available he was slotted straight into it. But he found creative work difficult and this meeting had made him realise how much he needed someone like Shanti to inspire him into taking greater risks.

Oh God how he yearned to take a few risks. And okay, this was only a newsletter, but the thought of even presenting these ideas to the UK and European CEOs seemed like a massive undertaking. However it was an undertaking that he somehow relished and he had surprised himself by ending the meeting by asking Shanti to present with him. Oh yes, and he had also asked her to have dinner with him that evening. Much to his delight, and amazement, she said yes.

They both left the room feeling very satisfied with themselves.

29

Terry decided to bite the bullet. He pressed the buttons on his phone that took him straight through to John Alexander, his champion at Phillips. John's strong, clear voice answered at the other end.

"Hi John, it's Terry again. Look I want to give you the heads up on the software problem. I know you're going to be getting pressure from above on this one so let's you and me keep the dialogue going, okay?"

Terry could feel a sense of strength growing inside him, particularly when John responded favourably to this suggestion.

"Okay John well here's where we stand. Our top technician Dima is out of the office until Monday. Now as far as I see it we're due to go live in three and a half weeks. François seems clear that this can still happen and without any glitches. But we won't have any further news on the problem itself until after Monday. I personally will give you a daily update on progress until we have sorted out the problem. If it looks like we might have any doubts about meeting the deadline then I'll let you know that too. How does that sound?"

John Alexander was happy. He felt he had enough information to appease his boss. He also felt satisfied that Terry had had the balls to communicate clearly and positively with him about the situation, even if he wasn't promising an answer right now to their problem.

He thanked Terry and Terry ended the call.

138

Terry stood up and could feel himself being able to take a deep breath. He couldn't remember when he had last breathed as deeply, but the realisation of it shocked him.

At the same time a rush of satisfaction swept through his body. All he had done with Alexander was be honest with him. He had told it to him like it was. He'd heard what the Coach had suggested to François and he had taken it on board and done it for himself. And it seemed to have worked.

Terry felt a smile stretching across his face. He felt so pleased with himself that he went up to Brenda to tell her personally that she would no longer have to deflect calls for him from anyone at Phillips.

"And that goes for Webbers too Brenda. Oh and anyone else you care to think of…" Brenda watched open-mouthed as Terry marched off triumphantly in the direction of François's desk.

"François, I've spoken to John at Phillips. The pressure's off there until Monday when Dima gets back. But I've promised him I'll let him know each day how we're getting on with sorting the problem, so don't let me down on this one. I'm going to go and talk to Mac at Webbers right now."

François's look of amazement mirrored that of Brenda's from the other side of the room.

The miracles were really happening.

30

The Coach felt confident and calm sitting in the room with a man whose manner many would find threatening and overbearing.

"James I'm going to make this very simple. If you want to experience positive, inspiring business results you've got to have a positive, inspiring group of employees. If you don't want to experience frightening, stressful business results then don't allow your business environment within which you all work to become frightening and stressful."

James Duncan was like a wounded animal. Every now and again he would go quiet and then would suddenly retaliate with a metaphorical kick, growl or grimace.

"This is not a frightening place to work. And as for stress—well all businesses are stressful—stress is good for you. It inspires people to achieve greater things." The CEO felt sure of his ground.

The Coach fixed him in his gaze again. "Are you sure James? Are you sure that stress is good for you? How do you know this? Oh I agree that challenge can be good for us, that it can inspire us to achieve greater things. But I believe it's when the challenge becomes too much, relentless, overpowering that it turns into stress and that an individual begins to suffer."

This was really getting to James Duncan. He couldn't give a monkey's about individual suffering and he certainly didn't buy into any of this new age claptrap about stress being bad for you.

"Look here, we all have to put up with a certain amount of stress. It's a fact of life. Get used to it." James was getting irate at this continued emphasis on stress.

"James, people can achieve amazing things when the right motivation is there; they can also create the most amazing messes when the wrong motivation is there. A holistic business approach is all about recognising that every single part of your organisation, from the cleaner to James Duncan himself, is equally valuable in the overall well-being of the company. And therefore their individual well-being is vital to the success of the company."

James Duncan had backed off for a minute. Whether he was just galvanising more strength to launch another attack or not the Coach didn't entertain. He continued to vocalise his train of thought.

"This approach also recognises that when all the members of the team come together to make the whole, the total of their joint contribution is much greater than the sum of their individual contributions. Something magical happens when the pieces fit together; just like in a jigsaw puzzle where the pieces really only make sense when they all come together to make the big picture."

By now The CEO was back up on his feet and wandering around the conference room. It was a technique that he had used over the years to unsettle people during negotiations. Over time it had become a habit and it manifested whenever he felt uncertain or uncomfortable. The Coach continued unfazed.

"Maybe you'd like to take a walk in the fresh air James before we continue with this." James suddenly realised what he was doing and sat right back down again in his chair feeling a little embarrassed.

"I'm sorry, I er felt a little cramp coming on..."

The Coach smiled again. He had such a knack of putting a person at ease. James relaxed a little more and decided to question his new colleague more on this interpretation of holistic business.

"So holistic isn't just about recycling your rubbish, drinking sugar free drinks and staff outings? What you're saying is that a holistic business recognises the contribution that every single piece of the jigsaw makes to the puzzle, no matter how small or inconsequential that piece appears to be?" James thought long and hard about the two questions he had just come out with.

The Coach didn't need to hurry any response. James knew that this was exactly what he was suggesting.

"Look James think of it like this. Let's take Brenda for example. She's probably the first contact that many potential clients have with the business. Now you don't need me to tell you how important first impressions are in life. And the first impression many people get of STF is as a result of talking to or meeting with Brenda. The fact that she has been here a little while also helps because it creates a sense of familiarity and continuity with returning clients or prospects.

"Brenda's calming voice over the years may have already kept you clients and made you money, and yet I bet she isn't even on a commission scheme is she?

"Or take the tech team. They are vital to the success of this company. They're coming up with— and maintaining—the product. Without these guys you have no business. And yet they are demotivated, feel undervalued and are totally stressed because they are permanently firefighting.

"They see salesmen on guaranteed salaries who can quadruple that in a year if they sell enough of the product and yet they, the very people who are expected to create and maintain that product, get stuck with occasional company perks such as your team building outings and a Christmas bonus. Is it any surprise there's resentment there?

"James, the days of thinking that you only reward your centre forward for scoring goals is long gone. The world is changing. If the team gets a good result, every member of that team—however large or small their role may have been—should receive some sort of recognition for their contribution. Even if they were on holiday when the actual deal was closed.

"Close a big deal and give everyone a share of the result. They don't have to be the same size shares but they do need to reflect that you are acknowledging the role that all employees make in the process of securing a contract. Not just the people who happen to be the public face of the company."

This was radical stuff that James was listening to. He had never heard such free-thinking ideas in his business life before. Imagine it, rewarding Brenda for instance when the Phillips' deal signed. I mean yes she had taken a lot of phone calls from them. She had even had to look after the whole accounts team when they came to discuss the numbers and he, Julian and Terry were still at another meeting. But to reward her for it? She got a salary, surely that was enough.

"James, see it from their side for a minute. The tech team for instance are on similar basics to the sales team and yet they see the sales team having the ability to multiply their incomes considerably just by doing their job well. If the tech team do their job well they get nothing; but if they screw up, well they get bollocked. Can you see how this might seem a tad dispiriting?"

James was thoughtful. "I suppose I'd never quite seen it like that." He paused a moment. "But we can't afford to give everyone the same size commissions we give our sales team. We'd go broke.

"I accept that James. But you could probably

engage with your sales team on this and explain what you want to do and see if you can't reach some sort of improved situation. They're team members, people love being part of a team. Ultimately this will mean the team will become stronger and win more business, whilst also taking a lot of the negativity out of the company that is currently leading to high levels of stress. Oh sure they're in it for the money, but if you can put this over to them that it could mean over time they'll end up making much more money and be less stressed—well they'd be fools not to listen. And they will listen to you James, you're a leader."

The Coach was in full flow. This was the big stuff, the reason he had got involved in business in the first place. To reach the decision makers and to help them to understand that the key to more effective business is not through harder work but through better management of the existing resources.

He knew his approach sounded simple—almost too simple—but he never made any apologies for this any more. The truth was simple. Create a happy, balanced and efficient working environment and you'll have happy, balanced and more effective results. Staff become more loyal because they are treated better; clients continue to supply business because they enjoy their dealings with you.

James remained quiet and thoughtful as the Coach continued with his teamwork theme.

"Look at it this way. You find yourself stuck in the jungle with a team of people with machetes. Your goal is to get out of that jungle as quickly as you can. The way most companies act at the moment, and the way STF is operating, what would happen is that everyone would start ploughing their own individual channels.

"One person would end up getting to the other side first leaving the others tired, sweaty and frustrated that their efforts were in vain. The successful person would find his or her celebrations marred by the resentment or feelings of failure of the others.

"But put them all together ploughing one channel—getting them to work together, taking rests, sharing the load—and at the end you will have a group of people with a great sense of satisfaction and self-respect for their own individual contributions as well as a great sense of the group achievement. And of course they will have reached their destination much more effortlessly than they would have done had they all gone by themselves.

"And that James is what holistic business is all about."

James looked up and the Coach could see that in that moment a penny had dropped. Sometimes it took the same words said over and over again but in slightly different ways for someone to come to a new understanding that would result in a change in their lives forever. Sometimes it could happen over months, other times over minutes. For some people one story could do the trick. For James Duncan, this simple analogy of the jungle had produced just such a quantum shift.

James felt a lightness that he had not felt for some time. He also felt the fear of what these words were implying. And he knew that even if he felt that some sort of group commission scheme would be beneficial, the Americans would never agree to it. And in that moment he felt stuck again, albeit not in a way that made him panic immediately.

"I need a cup of tea. Can I get you something er, what do I call you? I don't even know your name."

"You can call me Coach, James. And yes, thank you, a glass of water would be great."

James got up to leave the room. His legs felt different, slightly wobbly and he was distinctly light-headed. His stomach was busy gurgling away which it often did at times of high excitement. He walked out and paused as he entered the large open-plan office.

James surveyed the scene. He knew all these individuals pretty well by now. He looked at Brenda who, although busy answering calls, had immediately swivelled round on her chair the second she heard the conference room door open. He sensed concern in her face and tried to give her a reassuring look. He turned his stare towards the rest of the room. Shanti glanced up at him and he found himself smiling at her. She quickly returned her attention to her computer. In the tech area he could see François and Matt sitting opposite each other but seemingly completely oblivious to each other's existence. Matt looked up as well and caught James's eye. He also quickly returned his gaze to the screen.

But in those glances, with Brenda, Shanti and Matt, James experienced just what the Coach had described. There was a sense of fear in their expressions that James had previously seen as a sign that his leadership style was working. The last few minutes had made him realise that this was probably proof that the reverse was true; his fear-led approach was not working. It was just making people scared of him.

He could feel himself becoming more and more nauseous. He headed straight for the washroom which was outside the office next to the lift.

In the corridor he passed Julian walking past him with a very tasteful bunch of flowers. Julian—of all people. Julian of the bizarre bow ties. What a weird day this was turning out to be.

He just made it to the bowl in time.

31

"What's up with James?" asked the head of Accounts as he walked into the office with his flowers. Brenda responded simultaneously with a naughty glint in her eye.

"Oh Julian, thanks for the flowers, they're beautiful, you shouldn't have."

"Ha ha. They're for Serena, so keep your eyes off them Brenda! James—what's up with him? I just passed him in the corridor. He looked awful."

Brenda was fully aware of the quick exit that James had made. "Well, I don't know exactly, but I can tell you that he has just come out of a meeting with the Coach." She winked at Julian and they both took another look at the bouquet that he was holding in his hand before she continued. "And strange things seem to happen following meetings with him, don't they?"

They both laughed and Julian went to the kitchen to stand the flowers in a jug of water. He went back out to the reception desk and asked Brenda for a piece of A4 and a magic marker.

On the piece of paper he wrote in big capital letters "DO NOT TOUCH—JULIAN'S PROPERTY!" He stuck the sign to the flower bag and returned to his desk. As he passed the conference room he caught sight of the Coach. He was sitting with an immensely straight back in his chair with his eyes closed. He looked totally at peace.

Julian hovered for a minute or so. Shanti, on her way out of the office for her delayed meeting with the Frenfalls' PR team, joined him briefly in his spying. The Coach didn't move, didn't open his eyes. He barely even seemed to be breathing. They envied him this sense of apparent bliss in the midst of a bustling business environment. And they both silently decided there and then to find out more about what it was he was doing.

They were disturbed from their study by the sound of the main door opening. Seeing that it was a rather pale looking CEO returning they quickly went about their business.

153

Julian returned to his desk. What a weird day he thought to himself.

32

François was still feeling crap. At one level he was pleased that Terry had bought him some time; on another level though he was disappointed that he hadn't handled it himself. He was even more hacked off that he didn't have the technical skill to sort out the software problem.

He was just trying to get his head round what of his various 'to do' list he should focus on when he felt a tap at his shoulder. Oh shit. Matt. All he needed.

"Matt—wassup?" He'd made the expression his own since he'd first seen it on a TV ad years ago and he knew Matt hated it.

Matt felt his hackles go up. But he was determined to step through his resistance to tackling this face to face and so he spoke as calmly and clearly as possible.

"François, I've been doing some work in the last few weeks on this client log. I reckon it could really help us to avoid some of the hassles we're getting at the moment. You know, like now with Dima away, well no-one else can take over his accounts because we don't know what stage he's at with any of the software or web solutions. Nor do we know what he's said or to whom. And of course when a client wants to speak to him if a problem comes up they've got to wait until he's around again. It's crazy."

Matt had done really well to keep it calm but he felt his voice and body tightening towards the end of his little speech. François was immediately threatened by the term 'it's crazy' and took it as a slight on his tech team management skills. His ability to 'hear' Matt was stopped in that moment. His ego was just too much in control. He couldn't let himself accept help from his younger colleague.

He went through the motions as he had many times before with Matt. "Yeah, okay Matt, just ping it over to me in an attachment. I'll look at it as soon as I can."

Matt knew straightaway that his ideas would get the same treatment they had always got from François. Nothing. Well, either nothing or weeks later Matt would hear that François had presented a slightly altered version in his own words. He returned a little crestfallen to his desk.

He took a swig from his Coke. He looked at his client log presentation that he had completed a few days previously before the Coach had even appeared on the scene. It was good. Bloody good. And he knew it could not only help this company, but probably a load of other SME's as well.

His thoughts were interrupted by a small familiar sound that told him he had new mail. He looked at his inbox. His heart skipped a beat. She had replied.

"CU @ 7.30. HUGS XXX."

And his thoughts of business suddenly disappeared as he remembered that tonight he would be giving his fiancée some devastating news.

33

"James—are you feeling okay?" The tone of concern in Brenda's voice was quite genuine.

"Me? Oh, yes, thanks Brenda. I'm okay now thanks. Must have had something dodgy to eat. Brenda could you bring us a tea and glass of water into the conference room please?"

He was asking in a much softer voice than normal. Brenda was quite struck by the change in him.

"Brenda?" James called after her as she headed for the kitchen. He walked up to her and continued to speak softly to her. "Brenda, do you, er, do we…" James was fumbling for the right words. "Look, do you think we treat you okay? I mean—are you happy working here?"

Brenda knew in that moment that the Coach had got to him. And she also knew that it was important that she was honest and courageous with her response. She took a deep breath and spoke

157

quietly back to him.

"James, you know I've been very happy here and grateful for the opportunity I've been given. But you know what—now that you mention it—I do get pretty fed up with dealing with everybody's er, well how shall I put it…"

"Shit, Brenda?"

"Yes. I do get fed up with dealing with everybody's you-know-what. Basically James I feel like I'm being given really responsible things to do and yet I'm not being recognised for that. People seem to think I'm a human 'pooper-scooper'."

Brenda felt herself getting a little carried away and did not want to overstep the mark any further. She moved towards the kitchen and turned her attention back to tea preparation.

James Duncan muttered a taciturn "Thank you" and headed back for the conference room. There he found the Coach still in the state of relaxed alertness that Julian and Shanti had observed a few minutes earlier.

The CEO had sat down again before the Coach

opened his eyes. He smiled at James who had a thousand thoughts going round his mind.

"I er, don't quite know where we go from here Coach. Supposing you're right. Supposing this holistic approach you describe is the way to go. How on earth do we start implementing it?"

"Oh it's the way to go James. This is the business of the future. Once enough companies start operating in a truly holistic way, everyone else will have to follow. Because employees won't put up with anything less. They just won't work for a company that isn't valuing their well-being.

"Clients will also become a lot more choosy. They won't want to give their money and contracts to companies that are viewing their business in a short term way." The Coach spoke so calmly and clearly it was difficult to doubt the truth of what he said. He clearly believed this down to his very core.

"Okay. But like I said, what can we do practically to change the way we do business?"

The Coach looked directly into James's eyes. The CEO shuffled in his seat, such was the intensity of the look. The Coach spoke again.

"At the risk of sounding repetitive and new agey, *think holistically* James. In a holistic approach to life the outer state of the organism is reflective of the inner state. Someone who gets diagnosed with cancer for instance has had a breakdown going on inside for maybe weeks, months or even years beforehand.

"In business the outer state of your company is its dealings with clients, suppliers etcetera. The inner state is made up of the internal workings of the company—your staff and their relationships with each other.

"If the inner state is imbalanced, i.e. staff are stressed or not being heard or demotivated, then the outer state will be imbalanced. In other words performance will be poor. So the first place to look when you want to improve business results and long term sustainability is at the internal workings of the company, because the poor results or difficult client relations are purely reflective of a breakdown inside the company.

"James if all you ever get out of this meeting

with me is a kick up the backside to start looking at how you can really hear staff concerns and how you can create a more relaxed and supportive environment here then that in itself will have a massive impact upon Straight-Talking's performance.

"Take what's happening at the moment. You've got staff running round shit scared because there's a major problem with your software solution. You know it, your tech guys know it, your sales team know it. James even your receptionist knows it. And yet there is no concerted group effort to deal with it. Everyone's hoping it will either go away or that somehow they'll get through another day without having to deal with it.

"Now if we look at why no-one's dealing with this we'll find a simple answer. Everyone is scared to death of getting bollocked for screwing up. The sad thing is, the only reason they've screwed up is because they have been doing their job. Sales have been told to sell at all costs, not to question whether or not the product is any good. And the tech team have been so busy dealing with keeping up with problems that still exist in old software solutions they inherited that they have never had the chance to develop the new software before it was being sold as finished.

"None of this can happen in an environment where the team is being properly heard or where they feel safe to discuss problems and ask for help."

The CEO was totally silent throughout. Even his shuffling had ceased. He listened, he made notes, he fiddled occasionally with his fountain pen. The Coach was delivering a pretty stinging critique of his management style. It was hard not to take it personally. He thought of the brief conversation he had had with Brenda just before he came back into the room. She had been brave to share her thoughts with him and he had felt good that he had listened.

He sat there, more humble now than at any other point, making his notes and thinking. The Coach could see him struggling with it but could also see in him a real desire to try to engage with this process.

"So what about change itself? Surely not

everybody is ready to make changes?" His question was reflective of his self doubt as to his own willingness to change.

"One thing that blocks effective change James is the unwillingness to change. If someone, or a company as a whole, is willing to embrace change in all things then the potential is limitless. If change is viewed as wanted in only certain areas the potential is limited. Many people give up when they meet resistance."

James was getting interested. "Can you tell me of those members of staff you've seen today who is and who is not willing to change?"

The Coach knew exactly where James was going with this. "I can do. But I'm not going to tell you. I don't need to. It will become clear at the perfect time. Those who embrace change freely will display a measure of certainty, of courage and humility that you may not have seen in them before. They know they haven't got the answers to everything and will no longer pretend so often that they have."

James questioned the Coach again. "And those

who aren't willing to change? What about them?"

"Those people will generally continue to run into difficult situations and will not reach out to others to help. They will avoid making difficult phone calls, passing them onto 'juniors' to make instead and will bluff their way through meetings where they do not have the right answer.

"They will seek to control the behaviour of others through asserting their own dominance for fear that if they let others have control they will lose their standing. They don't want to be seen as helpless or needing assistance. Their inability to engage the support of colleagues in problem solving and their desire to assert their authority will eventually make their positions untenable."

James was quiet for a few moments. He recognised many elements of himself in the description the Coach had just given. Had he been unwilling to change? Was he using fear to control his staff? There was no doubt he found it difficult to ask for help. And he certainly always wanted to make the final closure on all deals rather than letting Terry do it.

164

Was that because he was scared of Terry gaining greater recognition than him?

The Coach could imagine the type of questions and thoughts going through James's mind. He let him reflect for a while before continuing.

"You see James, here's the killer. Business has to change. Not just STF, but business as a whole. It cannot expect individuals to sustain the high levels of stress that currently exist. The amazing thing is, much of this stress could be done away with. It's totally unnecessary.

"Neither will commerce itself survive in its present form if we do not start looking toward the longer-term view. The days of get-rich-quick-and-sod-the-future are over. At the risk of sounding totally PC, we need to be creating businesses that are gearing their focus towards the future well-being of their staff and the planet. Soon people just aren't going to continue to put up with any less.

"Are you ready for some real gold, James? Do you want to know the secret for the business of the future?" James mumbled an affirmative response.

The Coach continued. "The business of the future values two assets above all else. It constantly nurtures and protects these assets. What are these assets? I'll tell you James. You won't find them listed on any balance sheet. These assets are individuals and relationships. Why? Do you know why James?"

James didn't want to make a fool of himself by saying the wrong thing. He remained silent, just shook his head.

"It values the individuals and relationships above all else James because it knows that without individuals there are no relationships and without relationships there is no business."

James had heard enough. This final sentence from the Coach had been as much as he could take in one day. And the Coach knew it. James stood up and shook the Coach's hand, still feeling unsure as to whether to thank him or curse him.

"Do me a favour James. Let this all sink in for at least 24 hours before you decide to do anything at all. And if you do decide to start taking some action, make sure you start by taking the smallest of small steps first. Nothing else will be sustainable, and there is no need to hurry. It will all happen in the perfect time. Goodbye for now. I've really enjoyed chatting with you James."

With those words the Coach walked out of the Conference Room. He didn't stop to look back at the goings-on in the office, he knew he'd be back soon enough. On the way out he noticed a beautiful bunch of flowers in the kitchen with a big sign on them. He allowed himself a little smile. As he passed the reception desk Brenda, who was of course on the phone, managed to catch his eye and give him a look that suggested the magic was already beginning to happen.

34

By 5.45 pm that day James Duncan was one of the last left in the office. He sat at his desk staring at the calendar on the wall in front of him. The dates and scrawls merged into one mass of irrelevant details.

He needed a new view and decided that tomorrow he'd move his desk closer to the window.

Shanti had called from her meeting with Frenfalls to say it had gone on late but that she had some very exciting news that she'd share in the morning. Something about a joint publication venture with them. She sounded really uplifted. James was pleased, he'd always liked Shanti.

Julian—the most committed member of staff as far as time spent in the office was concerned—had left at 5.30 on the dot armed with the bunch of flowers that James had passed him holding earlier in the afternoon. There was a spring in his step as he left and a certain carefree look in his face that told James something good had happened to him too. And again James felt a sense of satisfaction that another member of his team was clearly feeling pretty okay. He had become unfamiliar with this feeling in recent months, but it told him once more how important the well-being of his team was to him.

François had also left about the same time. But he'd crept out, almost hoping not to be noticed. But now James knew why. His meeting with Terry, which had only finished at 5.00pm, had taken a turn he had not been expecting. Terry had told James how it really was with all the accounts and the software solutions. He'd described François's reluctance to delegate technical work to Matt for what he judged as a fear of surrendering his power. Hmm, well that was something James himself resonated with when he thought of Terry's selling ability and his own insecurity.

Terry had also explained the pressure that he had been under to make sales at all costs, even though the product wasn't ready—and the damage that would cause in his attempt to build up trust with his clients. And he'd explained that he was pissed off with chasing numbers when his talent for selling had been in building relationships and getting the big ones.

And, much to Terry's surprise, James had listened. James was taking on so much information in this one afternoon that he had felt like he had done three weeks work in a day. By the time the meeting ended Terry felt several pounds lighter. He sensed a wave of elation washing over him as he returned to his desk. An elation that the unveiling of the truth always brings.

James felt in some ways that he had been left holding the baby. About bloody time his wife would have said. He sat at his desk, still staring at the calendar. A tap on the shoulder disturbed him from his aimless thoughts. It was Brenda. Good old Brenda. His rock. The office rock.

"Goodnight James. Great day today huh? Some guy that Coach isn't he? Stroke of genius getting him in here if you ask me. Well done, quite a brave move I reckon." Brenda winked at him. "See you in the morning."

James was feeling so bamboozled by now he made no attempt to persuade Brenda otherwise.

Others had drifted out too in the last few minutes. The office felt different. People going home when the normal working days finish. This didn't normally happen at STF. It was like a fire sweeping through the office. By 6 o'clock only two people were left in the office, James and Matt.

James looked over at Matt's back. He was working quite intensely at his computer. Just at that moment he clapped his hands together and the printer started churning out some new document. Strange again, Matt was so often away on time.

James's direct line rang. It was his wife. "Yes, I'm leaving in a minute. I'll be back to tuck the children in tell them." He wasn't really thinking when he said it, he was still feeling completely fazed by all the information he was just beginning to absorb.

The phone went again. This time it was Shen Jacobs, the big boss. The biggest boss. The worldwide owner of STF, one of the richest men in America and someone you don't mess around.

He was clearly giving James some feedback on the visit. James responded in short, monosyllabic grunts. "Yes, I see, of course, good, fine, great...." It was nothing he hadn't heard before. But just before the call finished James had one thing to say to Shen.

"Shen listen, I guess I must thank you for sending the Coach guy in. I was a bit miffed at first, I would have liked to know he was coming. But, well I

171

can see now why it had to happen like this. He's, well, he's quite a character. Some good insights. Could help us. Where did you get him from?"

James clearly did not get the answer he was expecting. Not for the first time today his face turned quite ashen. He ended the phone call hurriedly and sat in his chair in a complete daze.

Shen Jacobs did not have the first idea who the Coach was.

Just as James was contemplating another extraordinary twist in an extraordinary afternoon, a beautifully presented document was placed on his desk in front of him.

"Proposal for Client Log procedure—designed by Matt Jenkins for Straight-Talking Finance."

Matt left his CEO with his project proposal and went off confidently to complete some other unfinished business with a certain lady. James looked down at the proposal. He smiled. A smile that started to stretch from ear to ear. He picked up the document to study on the train home, switched off the lights in the office and locked the door.

"A new idea is first condemned as ridiculous,
and then dismissed as trivial,
until it finally becomes what everybody knows."

William James

So What Happens Now?

If you now feel inspired to start creating the type of changes that you've been reading about in this book, either for yourself or within your company, log on to

www.barrydurdant-hollamby.com

or email welcome@barrydurdant-hollamby.com

If you'd like to be kept informed about future products involving The Coach or other products from The Art of Change, log on to

www.artofchange.co.uk

email welcome@artofchange.co.uk

tel +0044 (0)1342 823809

Author Barry Durdant-Hollamby can also be booked for talks and seminars – contact details as above.

Printed in the United Kingdom
by Lightning Source UK Ltd.
110520UKS00001B/82-516